SMARTER THAN AVERAGE GUIDE

JW
Guide to

Designing
Your
Retirement

Explore your options
Reimagine your identity
Create a fulfilling life

Set yourself up for a successful transition

JW Guide Guide to Designing Your Retirement

Explore your options

Reimagine your identity

Create a fulfilling life

Publisher's Note

JW Guide Guide to Designing Your Retirement

Published by Jake Willie

Copyright © 2023 Jake Willie

Cover by Santo K. Hadden.

Edited by Robert Wallace

JW Guide Guide to Designing Your Retirement

Get the guidance you need to excel at work from the most reputable company in the industry. The guides address your most urgent work-related concerns and are jam-packed with valuable how-to advice from top professionals.

The titles consist of:

A Handbook for Female Employees

The Manager's Guide to AI Fundamentals

How to Be an Excellent Boss

A Handbook for Increasing Productivity

A Handbook for Improved Business Composition

A Handbook for Improving Mental Health at Work

A Handbook for Formulating Your Business Case

How to Purchase a Small Business

A Handbook for Altering Your Career

A Handbook for Mentoring Workers

A Handbook for Cooperative Groups

An Introduction to Critical Thinking

A Manager's Guide to Data Analytics Fundamentals

A Manual for Handling Conflict

A Handbook for Giving Good Feedback

A Handbook for Planning Your Retirement

An Emotional Intelligence Handbook

A Manager's Guide to Basic Finance

A Handbook for Putting Your Plan into Action

How to Acquire the Necessary Mentoring

A Handbook for Landing the Ideal Job

A Manual for Completing the Correct Tasks

A Manual for Managing Groups

A Handbook for Better Decision-Making

A Manual for Improving Every Meeting

An Overview of Managing Adaptable Work

A Handbook for Handling Strategic Projects

A Handbook for Handling Stress at Work

A Manual for Managing Above and Below

A Handbook on Encouraging Individuals

A Manual for Getting Around the Toxic
Workplace

A Negotiation Handbook

An Overview of Networking

An Introduction to Office Politics

An Overview of Performance Management

A Handbook for Convincing Presentations

An Overview of Project Management

An Overview of Working Remotely

A Handbook for Formulating Your Plan

A Handbook for More Astute Networking

A Manual for Strategic Thought

A Manual for Developing Creativity

A Work-Life Balance Guide

A Handbook for Your Employment Search

A Manual for Developing Your Career

What you should know

a well-defined schedule. a relaxed dress code. leisurely mornings. It's time to work on your plan. What comes to mind when you think of retirement? Do you idealize it, envisioning how great life would be when you have no obligations and almost everything you do is optional? Do you overthink it, fearing you won't have enough cash, good health, or companionship to appreciate it? or in the midst of both? Although we are aware that there is no longer a single definition or age for retirement, is there still a framework or standard that we can rely on?

Whatever your definition of retirement may be, it's a significant life step for which you should plan and give careful thought long before you send your last "so long, keep in touch" email to customers and coworkers. However, a lot of us are too preoccupied with achieving our work objectives to consider what comes thereafter. Even when we do consider retiring, we often focus so much on the financial and health-related ramifications of aging that we neglect to consider the consequences for our sense of self. Early in life, we are taught that "planning for retirement" entails accumulating money and making prudent investments with it. Beyond the cliches about golf, card games, and tracksuits, however, nobody appears to be thinking about what retirement preparation entails. We understand that we won't be working forty or more hours a week, but how will we pass the time in a manner that makes us happy, gives us a sense of purpose, and enables us to give back? Will we cease all labor at once? Shall we launch the company of our dreams? Shall we take on a new role as a mentor, coach, instructor, or volunteer?

This book will assist you in adapting your interests, abilities, and experience to this new stage of life, whether you intend to wind down in the next five years, are just starting in your profession, or are retired and feeling lost. You'll discover how to:

What does retirement mean to you?

Determine options and routes that go beyond conventional retirement.

Create a connection between your new self and your former professional persona.

To increase your income, discover purpose, and give back, think about starting an encore job.

Proceed after an unexpected early retirement.

To integrate work skills into your free time and community involvement, use job crafting.

Use your skills and expertise for board service or consulting.

Talk to the people who matter most about your goals and aspirations.

Be proactive in reducing the stress associated with the change.

Develop new sources of meaning by embracing life's major issues, serving others, and forming connections.

Contents

The Key Life Changes That Surviving Pandemic Lockdowns Can Teach Us

We experience a three-part cycle that results in a long-lasting alteration.

How to Design an Improved Retirement

Start modest and have fun with it.

Retire with a goal in mind.

Create fresh sources of inspiration.

Acquire improved transition skills.

Yes, retirement is a significant shift. However, there is still more for you to do.

CHAPTER 3.

Evaluate your choices and future directions.

Arrange a Contented Retirement

You could use your previous talents in a new encore profession, but you're still you.

How to Determine Your Dream Career After You "Grow Up"

Whether your retirement is 10, 20, 30, or more years away,

Dealing with an Unexpected Job Loss If you didn't have time to prepare, here's how to start healing.

How to Use Your Retirement to Become a Coach or Consultant

independent work schedule, flexible hours, and the opportunity to impart your knowledge.

Are You Prepared to Take on Board Service?

Don't squander your knowledge and expertise.

The Retirement Handbook for Leaders

Give back, take your time, and plan your on-ramp.

CHAPTER 4.

Make Decisions

Selecting a Significant Alteration

Acknowledge and deal with prejudice to improve decision-making.

Emotions Don't prevent people from making wise decisions.

By recognizing your current feelings and your ideal feelings after a significant decision, you may make better judgments.

CHAPTER 5.

Retirement Is Difficult- Don't Try It Alone

Establish Your Board of Directors for Retirement

Figuring out what to do next requires teamwork.

Your Retirement and Your Relationships

Include the most significant individuals in your retirement narrative from the outset.

It Can Be Stressful to Retire

However, there are things you can do to make the golden years golden.

CHAPTER 6.

Set yourself up for success

How Are You Going to Assess Your Life?

You still have time to have a life you're happy with.

Introduction

Retirement is not an end, but a transition. Rethink and rework your retirement

People are redefining what it means to "retire" all across the globe. The traditional 65-ish goalpost is being replaced by a wide range of methods and occasions for leaving the realm of full-time, paid employment as we live longer, more fruitful lives. Retirement used to be a primary concern just for those of us in our 50s and older, but an increasing number of people in their early careers are considering whether or not to take a lengthy break before starting a new profession after their working lives.

People of all ages are asking themselves important questions these days about the kind of job they perform, how much work they do (if any), and the physical and psychological roles that work plays in their lives. Certain regions of the world have seen an increase in the number of people choosing to retire early. However, there are many other ways to reinvent our later years of employment, such as starting the business of your dreams, going back to school to learn a new skill, or getting hired back as a consultant at your previous employer. In these situations, you'll still get paid more and feel like you're truly valued. Frequently, instead of retiring to a life of leisure, we're picking up new skills, following long-standing or just discovered hobbies, and creating brands, companies, or portfolios that better reflect our beliefs and parental duties.

The tendencies we are seeing in our friends and family are supported by research studies, many of which are mentioned in the chapters in this book. A complete one-third of retirees ultimately reverse retirement and go back to work full- or part-time, according to Federal Reserve Board research. 1. The rise in older adults' workforce participation rates has even been noted by the Department of Work. 2. Merely 10.8% of those over 65 were employed in 1985. That figure is increasing and has almost doubled. In fact, according to Gerontological Society of America research, the fastest-growing demographic in the American workforce is those 55 and older. 3. This is partly the result of necessity: people in the lowest income levels are more likely to return to work after retirement due to rising living expenses and insufficient benefits. However, a higher number of wealthy retirees—35 percent—return to work in a professional capacity after a year or two to rejuvenate. This ratio is particularly higher at the highest income levels. 4 Some people describe retirement as working fewer hours or in a different capacity rather than as completely stopping employment.

The term "retirement" used to refer to the final years of our professions; however, there are now more possibilities than only voluntary work and artistic pursuits: Resuming full-time work, taking on gig work (the proportion of self-employed workers increases significantly with age), launching your own company (people 55 and older account for 21% of the US population, but they own a disproportionately high 50.9% of US small businesses, per survey data from 3,000 entrepreneurs), social entrepreneurship, or a combination of some of these options are among them.

The catch is that more individuals are choosing to work beyond the typical retirement age in new and innovative ways. However, it does not lessen the difficulty of transitioning to a new phase of life and career. The end of a "lockstep," three-stage existence, when a group of individuals of a certain age experience a brief learning phase (university), a lengthy working period, and a variable leisure period (retirement) at about the same time, has been celebrated by longevity.

In their book The 100-Year Life, Lynda Gratton and Andrew Scott argued that since we are living longer than when retirement was first proposed, it makes no sense to retire from a productive life while we are still at the peak of our abilities or to simply prolong the lengthy working years between our twenties and sixties. Rather, it makes more sense to switch between working, studying, and leisure time more regularly. For instance, Forbes claims that returning to school beyond the age of 50 is the new standard. Six Kevin, a 50-year-old submarine commander, is a prime example of this kind of jibe and tacking, as he wasn't prepared to leave the military. Having previously earned an engineering degree, he decided to go to law school and eventually became an attorney for the US Department of Veterans Affairs, assisting veterans with their appeals. He eventually rose to the position of judge before his second retirement, at the age of 74.

The absence of regulations is the new norm. Our lives may take on a plethora of phases. As we go, we're redefining retirement from the perspective of our parents. That's thrilling. and terrifying as well.

What This Book Is Going To Do

This book will assist you in developing a retirement plan that is specifically tailored to your abilities and interests. You may use it to make plans on your own or with your life partner. If you're already retiring and are searching for advice on potential next steps since you didn't have the time or resources to prepare ahead, this book will also be helpful to you. The concepts presented in this collection will assist you in determining what you want and how to go about obtaining it, regardless of whether you are choosing retirement on your terms or are subject to obligatory retirement regulations that give you little control over whether to make this move. While those who are getting close to retirement age might be the most likely to pick up this book, anyone at any age or stage of their career—even those in their early years—can consider retirement as a necessary stage of renewal in the increasingly nonlinear careers of today.

(As Well As What This Book Cannot Do)

This book won't teach you how to handle your finances when you don't have a reliable source of income or determine if you can afford to retire. This book won't assist you in evaluating your health or any current or potential illnesses that could restrict your options. This book won't assist you in navigating complicated legal paperwork when you terminate an LLC, dissolve a partnership, or create an estate plan. One of the first things you should do is consult with appropriate expert consultants in any of these areas where you may have concerns.

Make your way through the shift

Having devoted the majority of my professional life to researching various career transitions, including those that occur in the latter phases of our careers, I can identify three retirement-related insights that are reflected in the book's chapters: Transitions always have muddy middles, and the only way to go forward to a meaningful next phase is to try new things, make new connections, and tell new stories about ourselves. Retirement is a shift that tests your sense of identity.

Retirement is the process of transitioning from a known past working life to an uncertain future, not only an objective change of job or status. The "known" that becomes hazy and uncertain is your identity, or your sense of self. This is a result of the importance of work in defining who we are. Our time management strategies, the people we spend the majority of our waking hours with, and the narratives we tell ourselves and others about who we are and how we got there are all shaped by our work. Losing those anchors is hard, no matter how much we desire it or how much we prepare for that new chapter. You might consider how your retirement will affect your identity by reading through Section 1.

Second, a chaotic intermediate phase, an interim between the old and the new, when we often struggle because we're trapped in a maelstrom of competing demands, perplexing possibilities, and a generous helping of uncertainty, is the distinguishing feature of all transitions. This period may begin much earlier and continue for a considerable amount of time beyond the stated expiration date. However, it cannot be avoided. It is, in fact, a positive indication that we are addressing the major existential issues head-on. The untidy in-between is where a new you is formed. To put it simply, designing the ideal retirement requires more thought and time than closing doors. No suffering, no benefit. Because of this, the most frequent advice given to retirees is to avoid taking on any long-term obligations immediately. To choose what kind of future you desire, you need time apart from the chaos of your past life. You may define retirement for yourself in part two, and you can identify and assess your possibilities in section three.

Thirdly, the only way to go through a transition is to try new things, pick up lessons from them, and keep trying until you find the perfect next stage. You may prepare ahead of time, but you can't solve every problem in your brain. Three years later, it's not uncommon for even those who claim to know precisely what they want to do next—or what they never want to do again—to find themselves doing something quite different. Therefore, give up attempting to decide on a definite end point before you even start. Try out new positions, initiatives, and pursuits temporarily. Navigate through new networks to locate groups of peers pursuing similar goals as you, like-minded individuals, and "guides" who have been there before. Tell your tale to anybody who will listen, and as you get to know yourself better, make changes and revisions. You can reinvent yourself with these tools. You can obtain the assistance you need, make decisions, and make sure you're living according to your principles by reading sections four, five, and six.

This new life stage may give us incredible freedom to recreate ourselves on our terms and spend our time on what we desire to accomplish, assuming we are fortunate enough to be moderately solvent, generally healthy, and have supportive relationships (quite an order). However, a great deal of us still fear the inevitable shift, neglect to be ready, and end up getting trapped in the ostensibly secure past. With the guidance of this book, you may plan your retirement to make the remaining years of your life more meaningful, fruitful, and satisfying.

CHAPTER 1

What does retirement look like today?

Retirement for the Next Generation

Over 10,000 Americans reach the age of 65 every day. This was the standard retirement age for many years. People were expected to retire from their jobs and live a life of leisure starting in their early 50s, but most definitely by the time they were 70. Nevertheless, that paradigm has drastically changed in the last 20 years. Based on the findings of demographers Jim Oeppen and James Vaupel, Lynda Gratton, and Andrew Scott, the authors of The 100-Year Life, predict that half of today's 60-year-olds will live to be at least 90 years old. In the meantime, the days of government and business pension programs that ensured lifelong financial security are long gone. Many leaders are now reconsidering what it means to retire for these and other reasons.

Numerous scholarly investigations have been conducted to determine the best ways in which corporations may react to and benefit from this trend. Aging expert Ken Dychtwald coauthored an essay for HBR in which he suggested that businesses "retire retirement," fostering an environment that values expertise, permits flexible work hours, and offers exit strategies to retain senior employees.

Through our work with CEOs, we've also developed an interest in how people are preparing for retirement in the twenty-first century. We collaborated with York University's Jelena Zikic to interview one hundred managers and executives in depth who had either just retired or were actively contemplating retirement to examine the various approaches being implemented. For a more comprehensive understanding of retirement in the modern era, we also spoke with HR experts from 24 businesses in the financial services, natural resources, and high-tech manufacturing sectors— the industries where the majority of study participants were employed. We concentrated on managers because their exits have significant effects on the business and because they are more likely to be financially capable of choosing when and how to leave.

Contrary to what conventional theories and platitudes had led us to believe, we discovered a great deal more diversity in the beliefs and experiences of these people. We provide our results in this paper. Four guiding concepts that should assist individuals of all generations in navigating their late-career journeys have been derived from the insights gathered: Get ready to deviate from the plan, discover your retirement metaphor, strike a new agreement, and change the world.

Get ready to go off-script.

As we listened to managers share their experiences, we found that relatively few had decided to go from full-time employment to retirement at a certain age or eligibility. Their careers came to an end in a variety of ways, often on erratic schedules. Although some managers did talk about "following the [traditional] script," others spoke about "identifying a window" of opportunity when retirement felt right; "having an epiphany" because a shift in priorities away from work was brought on by health issues or other events; "cashing out" with a sizable package; "becoming disillusioned" by organizational changes; and "being discarded"—that is, being forced out of a position or establishment. All in all, a lot of things had an impact on how their retirements turned out.

Take 56-year-old Louis, who had worked for his employer for 32 years as the general manager of a sizable division of an international telecommunications corporation. When his company named a guy he didn't regard as the new CEO, he made the unexpected decision to leave early. Louis thought that he could go as soon as possible, even though he remained on for two years to assist with a restructuring. Alan, a 49-year-old regional sales manager for a manufacturing business that enjoys success and respect, had a similar experience. He was offered three alternatives after the ownership and restructuring of his company: an early retirement payout, a demotion, or a lateral shift requiring a geographic relocation. He decided it would be better to take the package, even though at first he thought he was too young to retire.

We should all prepare to improvise and adapt since very few of us will have total control over when and how our careers finish. Although they may not result in an instant departure, mergers and acquisitions, changes in management or strategic direction, restructurings, and unanticipated personal crises can all start the process. Regardless of how well you've planned for retirement, there's a strong risk that things won't work out precisely as you had intended.

Discover Your Retirement Metaphor

When discussing retirement, managers utilize a range of terminology. Some refer to it as a downshift from a difficult profession, as a detox from work-related stress, or as freedom from the daily grind. All of those analogies perfectly capture Jim's experiences. A health concern forced him to resign from his role as CEO of a multinational corporation when he was only 50 years old. Jim didn't want to end up like his father, who passed away in his thirties. Some see an opportunity for change or a rebirth in their lives. Consider Margaret, who quit her rigorous position as an executive-in-residence at a prominent business school to take on a challenging role in marketing and strategy planning at a consumer products firm. Others see retirement as a turning point in their work, fear losing their sense of self, or see themselves sticking with it and using their abilities in the future. A prime example of the latter is Bill, a geologist who, after working for an oil business for 25 years, chose to create an oil drilling company with a friend and retire early.

However, people's views about retirement often change as they get older. Some people who at first saw it as, for instance, liberation—the ability to go on cruises, play bridge, or go golfing—can transition into modes of staying the course, transformation, or renaissance. Go over the remainder of Jim's narrative. While his first years of retirement were spent relaxing and recuperating from a demanding profession, he also started to miss certain parts of his successful career. Prioritizing his family, he finally returned to his career as a mentor for aspirational young managers.

According to our study, people may create a retirement that feels good for them if they have a flexible mindset and are open to switching between metaphors. Thus, give it some thought and consider what it means to you, particularly if you're about to go through this significant life step. What pictures come to mind? Which of the analogies we've discussed resonate with your goals and aspirations, if any? Is there another route you should take if none of these speak to you? Gaining a deeper understanding of who you are, how you see your life and career, what kind of person you want to be in the future, and all the various identities and activities you might pursue are all part of the goal.

Additionally, keep in mind that you have other options after you retire. Future generations will value such adaptability even more. Gratton and Scott estimate that an individual turning 20 today has a 50% probability of living to 100, whereas an individual turning 40 has the same chance of surviving to 95. Even if you retire at the age of 75, you should experiment with several retirement options.

Make a new deal.

Many professionals are making agreements to remain at their businesses with modified schedules or duties rather than retiring entirely. Consider Daniel, a top executive at a financial company who worked out a deal to stay on the job part-time. He now withdraws for two weeks every month to a fishing and hunting hut in the wilds along the coast. However, Daniel spends the remaining two weeks back at corporate headquarters, serving as a mentor to upcoming executives and a "thought leader." A third experienced manager who took part in our research suggested a three-way task split between two coworkers who had small children. His colleagues wanted to continue growing their careers on family-friendly schedules; he wanted to take a step back while being involved, and their high-tech company approved the proposal.

Executives often choose a phased retirement strategy, gradually cutting down on their work hours while assisting in the transfer of knowledge and accountability to their successors. For example, Mark, a senior forestry executive, arranged to work 60% of his duties after attaining pensionable retirement age. In this manner, he could continue to support his company—most notably, by serving as a mentor to two teams of managers and aiding in succession planning—while also attending to some urgent health concerns. Gradually, he reduced his work hours.

Making arrangements for contract employment with a previous employer is an additional option. These agreements are advantageous to the company (which may regain lost skills) as well as the personnel (who get remuneration and the chance to reengage). Peter was a mid-fifties banker who was requested to return on a contract basis to fill a post needing his special knowledge of small-business loans six months after he had retired.

Adam took yet another route out, asking for a two-year leave of absence to accept a job as a municipal councilor when he was in his early fifties. After briefly returning to his company, he officially resigned from it at the age of 56 and went on to become the director of a large community group.

We urge everyone thinking about retiring to investigate their options for remaining or departing. Examine your work closely, your distinct background, abilities, and expertise, as well as your employer's perception of you.

Think back to the different positions you've had, the tasks you've accomplished, and the situations in which you felt most fulfilled and contributed the most meaningfully.

There could be more leeway than you would expect for creative, one-of-a-kind job positions or arrangements, even if not all businesses can support them. Inform your supervisors or human resource managers about the concept informally after you have a clear understanding of the contribution you would like to make and your desired timetable. If they won't look into flexible possibilities for you to remain on or go, or if they won't give you what you need, think about contacting other organizations; they could be happy to provide that flexibility.

Make An Impact

Retirement has long been associated with charitable endeavors, maybe as a result of heeding Andrew Carnegie's maxim that one should spend the first third of one's life learning, the second third building wealth, and the last third giving the money away. However, we discovered that a large portion of today's retirees contribute to society in ways that go well beyond money. Several instances include: Harry, an engineer turned plant manager in the pulp and paper business, began working with high school dropouts to assist them in gaining employable skills when he was abruptly dismissed in his early sixties. After retiring from a bank at the age of fifty, Linda, a specialist in management training and development with 28 years of experience, returned to school to get a degree in international development to open an orphanage for African children who had lost their parents to AIDS. A brilliant investment banker on the verge of burnout, Sylvia decided to retire early and accepted a significant (unpaid) position as treasurer of a significant cultural institution's board. Former telecom executive Gary quit to create a new business that would provide funding to socially conscious businesses.

It makes no sense to put your skills on hold in retirement when your expectations are higher for a longer lifespan and greater mental and physical health. The trend going forward will undoubtedly be for retirees to use their knowledge, expertise, and skills to improve their communities or the wider globe. This is particularly true for the socially concerned Millennial generation. If you're sick of the particular task you've been doing, there are plenty of other things you can accomplish with your leadership, collaboration, and project management skills. Retirement is a beginning rather than a finish; it's a chance to try new things, pursue interests you have, and maybe even create a legacy of your own.

How Retirement Modifies Your Identity and Life, along with two strategies to help you get through it

both prosperity and well-being. When individuals approach the conclusion of their working careers, those two things are often on their minds. Is retirement within my means? Will my health allow me to fully enjoy it? According to research, individuals are much happier in retirement when they can provide positive answers to those two questions.

That should come as no surprise.

However, after quitting their job permanently, individuals often find themselves with more questions. Now, who am I? What even do I tell folks when they ask what I do?

We identify so much with our work. Retirement fundamentally unshackles us from our self-concept. Additionally, recent research guides how to manage this shift more skillfully.

120 professionals from three distinct firms throughout the United States were questioned by researchers from MIT Sloan School of Management (Lotte Bailyn), Bentley University

(Marcy Crary), Harvard Business School (Teresa Amabile), and Questrom School of Business (Kathy Kram and Douglas T. Hall).

The research focused on the changes that retirement brings about in terms of psychology, society, and relationships. They also discovered that identity bridging and life restructuring are the two main processes that retirement initiates.

Teresa Amabile discussed the study's conclusions with Curt Nickisch, presenter of HBR IdeaCast. She oversees that group of scholars and is a professor at Harvard Business School in semiretirement.

HBR: Did your desire to do this stem from the fact that you were nearing or already in retirement?

Teresa Amabile: Unquestionably.

In what way?

When I started thinking about the research a few years ago, my husband started telling acquaintances that I wanted to retire with an evidence-based plan. And I suppose it is! For my part, I was very interested in how others went about it and what constitutes a fulfilling retirement.

As a professional who studies organizational behavior and how people experience life and work, I was also considering retirement. According to my earlier study, individuals are happier at work on the days, weeks, and months when they believe they are moving forward with important tasks.

What happens when you stop doing that important work? There are those folks in my family, friends, and coworkers who just can't seem to put their work down. They are unwilling to go through that change.

It feels a lot like being run over by a train, but at least a train has direction and velocity.

Indeed. Every day at work is filled with a feeling of accomplishment; even on the most stressful days, you've typically accomplished something. You feel that your life is moving forward, and you know where that track is headed, so your train metaphor is fascinating.

When you get off the train, you're in the unknown. and it may be very frightening. Some people get enmeshed in that terror. Some people, nevertheless, seem to be able to board and investigate new trains. In my opinion, such individuals were typically content with their lives both throughout the transition and the early years after retirement.

It seems that a lot of individuals spend a long time deciding what they want to accomplish next.

We studied the first five to seven years of retirement, particularly the first year and a half, as well as the immediate pre-retirement phase. Some begin planning their future post-career lives of retirement. That is not typical. For some individuals, the move to a more secure existence might happen in a matter of months. I watched a few individuals for six years after they retired, and after three of those years, one of them continued to feel unsatisfied with his retirement.

It defies logic since, on the one hand, you have always known that you would take this action. For decades, people have had retirement fantasies. And then to claim that you still don't know what you're doing or how you want to spend your time three years into retirement. That doesn't seem like it ought to be occurring.

It's challenging in part because a lot of our fantasies center on money. People dream of being free of the strain and stress of their jobs, without a doubt, but they also dream of being financially secure. You know, you think things would go easily if you had a nest egg. People may not be aware of this, but for decades I have spent the majority of my waking hours doing something, and soon I will need to find something else to do with my time.

Thus, life reorganization is one of the two major processes that we have examined in our study. The day you leave the workplace for the final time, you have to rearrange your life. Regardless of whether you worked full-time or part-time before retiring, you will need to adopt a new strategy for living.

Identity bridging, a collection of behaviors individuals take part in to preserve significant facets of their self-identity throughout the retirement transition, is the second key process we've identified in our investigations.

First, I would like to inquire about life restructuring. What is meant to be understood by "being an architect," as you and your coauthors put it in your research?

The main settings of your life are referred to as your life structure; these include the actual physical locations where you spend most of your time, the main activities you participate in, and the most significant interpersonal connections.

Much of it disappears when you're not working.

Those who are retiring are asked, "Do you miss working? Most of us are unaware of how crucial anchoring those professional ties is, so we say things like, "I don't miss the work, but I do miss the people."

We also underestimate the significance of the work structure. For many years, we have been living as if we were occupants of a life building that our organization had constructed for us. At nine in the morning, we know where we're headed. We essentially know what we're going to be doing and who we're going to be engaging with Monday through Friday.

What we intend to consume... what food we will eat and where we will consume it. Our weekends are likewise planned around the 9–5—or whatever the hours are—that are in place Monday through Friday. We can dedicate a day or a portion of a day to doing all the tasks that we were unable to complete throughout the workweek.

"You know, my life structure now is that I have Sunday—Church Day—followed by Saturday, Saturday, Saturday, Saturday," said one of our retirees.

Yes, there are 300 Saturdays in a year.

Indeed. Amazingly, I can do whatever I want, but it's also really unsettling. You must consider where you will spend your time and how you will organize it. People must complete four activities to restructure their lives. We refer to these duties as developmental because they play a significant role in the adult development of individuals who have worked for a significant portion of their lives.

Choosing to retire is the first step. Choosing when and how to retire is a choice related to life structure. Do you want to start working a part-time job at your current place of employment and eventually leave? But that's not merely a choice related to employment. It also concerns your relationships, since the majority of individuals in our survey are in partnerships. They share their lives with a spouse or other important person.

In your investigation, you tell the tale of a married couple's husband who, after retirement, returns home and alphabetizes the spices.

One of our best instances was the guy who said he drove his wife crazy because she was the one who took care of the house. For some baby boomer couples, such is the case. After not spending much time together on weekdays for maybe thirty or forty years, she had her structure to her life, and now this person was invading it.

The man said, "The day I retired, I organized all the spices alphabetically, and she left for her volunteer work." They agreed that he would be someplace else when she told him, "You need to get out of this house for at least four hours every day." She just cared that he found himself something to do; she didn't care where it was.

He thus set up a regular breakfast rendezvous with neighbors and sought some volunteer work. However, some haggling with his partner was required. We're discovering that often.

Releasing oneself from employment is the second developmental challenge. Some people leave on their final day as if they were just removing their bag, putting it down, and walking away. It's not that simple for a lot of individuals.

Are they picking up the phone to make a call to their colleagues? Yes, or skulking around social media in an attempt to learn what's going on at work. Alternatively, they continue to rise at five in the morning, and after breakfast, they use their computers to check their emails just like they used to when they were employed.

Others find it difficult to move on mentally. They feel as if they are still in the workplace even when they are not actively working on it. They think about it often.

Investigating and testing a novel, temporary retirement life structure is the third developmental task. Managing the transitional period between feeling at ease in your pre-retirement life and at ease in your post-retirement life is the main focus of this assignment. Liminal refers to being between two points in time or in the middle of a transition. There are several approaches that people take to this. Some people make elaborate plans, while others brainstorm many ideas without coming up with any concrete ones. One of the individuals we spoke with discussed some thoughts he had before he decided to retire.

Serving as a senior project leader for the organization, he firmly believed that he had developed a great deal of experience. He said, "You know, I feel like I could teach a course on project management or maybe write a book about it as a way to give back."

Well, by the time I spoke with him five years after his retirement, neither the book nor the teaching had taken place. He enjoyed being lazy once he retired, which is what occurred with the book and the course, as it does to many of the folks we've interviewed.

Although some people use the term "lazy" to describe themselves, I shouldn't use it myself. "What's the best thing about being retired so far for you?" was the question we posed after the conversation. Unexpectedly, many respond without hesitation, "Not waking up to an alarm clock," and many more will state that having the ability to arrange their day however they choose is the greatest part.

or not.

or not. And since that independence feels so nice, people avoid committing, particularly one as grandiose as this. This leads us to another discovery of ours: almost all retirees experience extreme happiness straight away, ranging from extreme satisfaction and contentment to outright euphoria.

An enormous load just disappears.

The absence of commuting is a huge benefit for a lot of individuals. There are no worries about spending the day battling fires or not finishing everything on their to-do list. Some people find that the lack of structure is so enjoyable that, six months or even a year later, they find themselves reluctant to volunteer for things they wanted to do and still want to do because doing so would require them to commit specific hours to the organization, and they don't want to be bound by that. But shortly after the first phase of feeling like they're on vacation, others require some order in their days. One gentleman, for instance, who loved riding, managed to get part-time work at a bicycle store. He called it his "landing spot," referring to the moment he took a big step forward in his profession.

This study has shown us that it's important to consider our goals rather than focusing just on solving the financial problem. However, since it involves such significant mental retraining, it seems like you won't understand what it will be like until you get there.

Yes, it is. Everything changes. The last of the four developmental tasks comes after the liminal period and involves consolidating a new, somewhat stable living structure. Many of the individuals we spoke with had reached a stage in their lives where they were content with their new structure and believed it was working. And the feeling of urgency that once pervaded me—that I needed to sort out my life—has vanished. There was a feeling of having found a comfortable rhythm in life.

That is the period of consolidation that we refer to. For some individuals, it might occur within a few months after retirement. Usually, it lasts between six and a year. Sometimes, even after three or four years, the individual still doesn't feel as if they fully understand their new life pattern.

That's why it's fantastic if an organization offers a program that allows employees to work part-time as they prepare for retirement.

It's what you're carrying out.

Yes, that's what I'm carrying out. It's fantastic because it lets you enjoy that flexibility and independence for a large portion of your workdays—not all of them, but a large portion of them.

It's not like you're quitting entirely.

Since you're not making the switch abruptly, you may experience what it's like to be at home on a day when you would typically be at work. What kind of interactions do I wish to have with this other resident of the house? And would I want to give a few hobbies a try? Numerous retirees in our research choose to unwind and enjoy their independence and flexibility for a few weeks or months, which may be an excellent way to start retirement. Subsequently, they began interacting with people at volunteer placements and became more involved in their communities. Alternatively, they began to devote more time to a hobby they had enjoyed before retiring, or they ventured into a new activity that had always piqued their interest. From these activities, great new friendships would often blossom.

However, you discovered that these questions—who am I?—have made it very difficult for some individuals to make the move to retirement. How am I acting? What skills do I have?

Would you mind answering one of the interview questions we used with participants in our study? Which would you rather say: Your job defines who you are or what you do?

I have conflicting emotions regarding the idea that my job defines who I am, but I would argue that it does. Looking back on my career, I think I was a little too sluggish to take advantage of possibilities because I felt like I belonged in the job and the organization.

Looking back, I realized that I was taking advantage of the firm more than I ought to have. I believe that my upbringing had some influence on some of this. Because my father was a career army officer, I have a strong sense of obligation to carry out my responsibilities.

and maybe allegiance to such a group.

Yes. Striking the correct balance has been difficult.

Your thoughtful response does, however, provide a little window into how individuals conceptualize identity. A significant number of the participants in our research—all professionals and knowledge workers—strongly identify with their jobs, professions, organizations, and coworkers.

How would you handle that? When you retire, what do you do with that large portion of yourself? We've found that a lot of individuals participate in a practice known as "identity bridging," which is essentially preserving or strengthening a significant part of oneself before retirement. Our results imply that you might benefit from identity bridging if you could identify deeply with your job and feel that it represented a significant portion of who you were. One significant method that some individuals use to do that is by really bridging a gap in the worker's identity.

This entails volunteering and working for a nonprofit.

Yes, it is one approach to it. One individual we spoke with felt that a key component of his professional identity had been serving as a leader in his organization. By accepting a volunteer leadership position in the church where he had long been a member, he bridged that identity and carried it into his post-retirement life. When we asked him to list a few characteristics that best encapsulated his essence, he cheerfully responded with the term "leader," since he found this to be quite fulfilling.

As one of our respondents did, other individuals could establish their own one-person consulting business as a means of bridging their professional identities. She coached new hires in her last position before departing from her company. She found her vocation very late in her career, but she liked it so much that she thought it was her calling. She thus decided to concentrate her part-time, post-retirement consulting firm on mentoring young managers and business owners.

A few more participants in our research began their businesses. For one such individual, the worker persona had been crucial, and he feared leaving full-time employment and being unemployed. Because of how terrifying it may be, many people have referred to this as "jumping into the void" or "leaping off the cliff." After retirement, this gentleman launched a handyman company. When he was a high-level IT professional, he always enjoyed doing home repairs. What do you know? I can take care of my friends, neighbors, and community members in this way.

He therefore really established a small LLC. He produced business cards on paper. He wasn't charging much, and he wasn't devoting a lot of time to this task each week. But when others inquired about his work, he managed to answer anything other than what he feared to hear—"Oh, I'm retired." Instead, he was able to add, "Oh, I have a handyman business." It was essential to him to have that physical item; therefore, let me offer you my card. It was similar to securing employee identification with a material object.

For others, it is not their job identity that serves as the crucial identity that spans the retirement transition. It's about growing or improving a non-work-related component of their identity that they had when they were employed. One of the most frequent patterns we've seen is that individuals who loved their hobby before retirement become significantly more involved in it after retirement. One guitar-loving retiree, for instance, joined a band after retirement and quickly expanded on his identity as a musician. It may be very rewarding and pleasurable to bridge those identities. A retired individual may sometimes concentrate on a connection that they had before retirement and that had a significant role in shaping who they are now. They are now strengthening that involvement and spending more time with that person.

One of our retirees, for instance, mentioned how essential his father's identity had always been to him. One of his three children was still living at home when he retired. She was a senior in high school and was having some difficulty in her academic career as well as in a few other areas of her life. They were close, but he worked so hard that they didn't get to spend much time together since his profession took up much of his time.

After retirement, he was considerably more involved with her. He gave her homework assistance. Together, they worked on projects. It bridged the gap between his father's identity, which had previously been a small but significant aspect of his identity, and greatly enhanced his life. It now takes up a significant portion of his identity.

You also speak about individuals who bring up memories from their past, such as a person who used to adore hot cars and then purchased one just before retiring. Is this the quintessential retirement project? Indeed! That's known as waking up a dormant identity. Before the demands of work and climbing the corporate ladder, this individual had been an active hot rodder. Additionally, early in his career, his wife pleaded with him, pointing out that they had little children. You're taking part in a risky activity. Do not enter those hot rod races, please.

And so he did sell his hot rod. Then he purchased a new one as he was getting ready to retire.

What stands to lose for me?

Indeed. He liked becoming back involved with the hot rod world and going on group rides; his wife told him to "go for it, baby." For him, it was a lovely way to connect his identities.

It often comes down to raising those things. But given that you speak of gaining as much as possible by climbing the corporate ladder, I wonder whether this is a failure of corporate America. or that folks just don't have the time for it. You may certainly plan for retirement more effectively, but isn't it also part of the problem that businesses require their employees to function in a manner that leaves them with little to no personal identity when they leave the company? Indeed. Our job nearly always embodies a great deal of who we are. Our job takes up so much mental space that we allow other aspects of ourselves to deteriorate. My culinary abilities have utterly deteriorated, partly because I have an amazing spouse who is a gourmet chef and whose work is less stressful than mine.

Interestingly, what we've seen in our interviews is that those who can continue being creative outside of work, even when they're completely focused on their profession, tend to benefit from this, as it's something they can develop later on. It provides a connection to their inherent selves.

In what ways has this study altered your retirement plans? I've been allowing myself to dedicate time each week to my avocations, which include being a grandma, in addition to the time I love to spend on this study.

Writing is one of my other interests. I've been attempting to write and read more poetry lately. In addition, I've been strengthening my bonds with my five sisters, my husband, and our kid. All of it has enhanced me.

What will you tell people when you retire?

I'll introduce myself as a retired Harvard Business School professor and let them know what else I'm up to at that point.

CHAPTER 2

Make your retirement plans.

Architect a Retirement That Inspires You to Extend Your Options

The staff at George Thorne's Austin, Texas, medical office greets him pleasantly and strikes up a chat about children and dogs. Having worked as an ophthalmologist for over 30 years, he is quick to express gratitude for his patients, colleagues, and team. He has enjoyed his work. However, he just decided to phase down his practice entirely and cease doing surgery at the age of 65. With a tinge of agony, he said to me, "I don't know what's on the other side of this, but it's time."

George resembles a lot of the baby boomers whom I tutor professionally. Their personalities have been fundamentally shaped by their successful and gratifying high-profile occupations. They are prepared—or compelled—to leave their long-standing careers as they get closer to the so-called retirement age, but many are also a little worried about what comes after. Their worries are more about identity and transition than money.

How can I effectively remake myself as I leave my work behind? How does the following stage seem to me? How can I prevent myself from being bored?

I used to make jokes with my buddy Aaron, like, "Ask a baby boomer about retirement if you want to provoke them." The R-word causes allergies in a lot of boomers. The explanations make sense. Many people associate retirement with a binary off-switch regarding golf, bingo, and death. It implies a set location, while 21st-century reality is much more flexible and individualized.

So I advise folks like George to see this effort as constructing your next phase rather than framing it as retirement planning. This is more than simply a charming phrase. This arrangement, in my opinion, makes the process more powerful. It changes the mood by emphasizing that they are in control, expanding the scope of alternatives, and giving the impression that it is an evolving process rather than a definitive one. Plus, it's more enjoyable. You get to create this reinvention; you don't have to prepare for retirement.

Here are some pointers to help you have a more enjoyable and seamless experience while creating your next step.

Call it by name.

When this happens, one of the first things I ask folks is what they would want to name it. Which term should we use while discussing it? Some people continue to live into retirement. Some think of names with a theme, such as "playtime," "encore career," or "giving back."

My buddy Craig had a successful global corporate career before resigning from his position as CIO of a Fortune 100 business two years ago. Even though he is no longer employed in the conventional sense at age 63, he does not see himself as retired. He travels, spends time with family, and assists with political campaigns in addition to offering advice to early-stage enterprises. He describes this era of his life as his "repurposing phase" in response to my question. For

For Craig, the "repurposing phase" is preferable to "retirement" since, in this chapter, he values being involved and changing the world. "I enjoy receiving phone calls," he said. "I want to feel like I have something to offer."

The first step to taking charge of the next chapter and making it your own is naming it. Although it may seem to be a cheap obfuscation, this is not the case. You clarify for yourself what this next stage implies by labeling it in terms that are meaningful to you. Everyone doesn't need to understand the name. All it has to do is make sense to you.

Allow time for you to slough off old skin.

An executive vice president called me two weeks ago to inform me that she had just been let go due to a merger. She responded, "They told me yesterday." "I'm not sure what I'll do next. Perhaps retirement is in order. I'm not sure.

"Maybe it would be beneficial to give this some thought before deciding what to do next?" I answered. "How about you go hiking or something, and we can discuss it in a few weeks?" She sent me an email yesterday from the Oregon Highlands. She did follow my suggestions! She wrote, "I didn't realize how much I needed this."

Many individuals try to push through the transition when they leave a fast-paced profession. It's as if they think becoming busy or making a big commitment would make them feel less lost and confused when they get off the treadmill.

Rather, give yourself time and room to process the experience and get rid of your old skin. Accept that you will have a period of mourning for your former self. There are phases you will go through; it's not like turning on a light switch and finding yourself in a bright new chapter. (To help you brainstorm, go to the sidebar under "4 Questions to Help You Plan Your Retirement—or Your Next Act.")

As previously noted, Craig departed his position as CIO and granted himself six months "without pressure to be productive." He said, "It was one of the best things I did." He gave himself time to heal, as he understood that losing his former identity would take time.

Imagine your brand-new environment.

The "wheel of life" is one resource that I find useful throughout change. Eight slices on this pie-shaped wheel stand for several aspects of life: career, spouse, physical environment (house), fun, health, money, friends, and personal growth. Writing down your vision for each area as you move through it is a helpful exercise. Where would you want to take them in your transition, and where are you at right now in this regard? Engage your partner or spouse in the process, if you have one. After all, reinventions are a team sport.

If your retirement plans require you to earn a certain amount of money, that requirement comes first and will probably restrict your possibilities. In particular, you'll probably need to keep working full-time (since such jobs are often more lucrative), and you may need to stay in the field where you've spent most of your career because you'll get paid more for your seniority and expertise. But if obtaining a high wage isn't essential, there are other things to think about.

How much freedom from the place are you looking for?

You should consider how to create a location-independent retirement if you see yourself juggling a little bit of employment with a lot of travel or if you would like to spend the winter in a warm climate. Maybe you decide to take a career (like teaching or teaching at a university) that is part-time and gives you flexibility for the rest of the year. Alternatively, you could choose to concentrate on occupations that allow you to work remotely or in a hybrid environment (such as becoming a freelance writer or consultant). When it comes to landing the position in the first place, having a strong network of connections may be more important than your actual location.

What kind of change would you want to see?

You have a few simple alternatives if you only want to downshift from your present field but are still interested in it. One is to talk to your present employer about the potential of switching from a full-time position to a consulting one, maybe working a few days a week, or concentrating on other projects.

on a particular project. With a guaranteed income before you leave, that might make the move to retirement easier. As an alternative, maybe you have connections in the sector who might be interested in hiring you as a consultant. You'll need to start building the foundation early since you'll probably have fewer connections in your new field if you're searching for a bigger transition and want to leave your present field behind.

How can you put your future career on trial right now?

In my book Reinventing You, I tell the story of Patricia Fripp, a hairdresser by trade who fell in love with public speaking. Originally honing her craft on the side, she gave presentations at hair shows. Eventually, several of her corporate hairstyling clients asked her to speak to their staff on sales and customer service. She was passionate about speaking, but she also recognized that trying to support herself full-time through speaking would be hasty. Rather, she had rented her hair shop for ten years, so she made a long-term strategy to increase her speaking engagements so that, when her lease was up, she could easily move into her new career. And that's exactly what she accomplished. The more time you prepare, the more leeway you have to take risks and explore new avenues while maintaining the stability of your monthly income.

In retirement, many individuals want—or need—to continue working, preferably by accepting a challenging position that allows them to develop personally. By pondering these issues and preparing for your next deed as soon as possible,

If it's feasible, you may smoothly move on to your next significant task.

———————

Dorie Clark is a keynote speaker and marketing strategist who teaches at Duke University's Fuqua School of Business. Thinkers50 has recognized her as one of the world's top 50 business thinkers. The Long Game: How to Be a Long-Term Thinker in a Short-Term World is her most recent book.

Another easy practice that is surprisingly effective is to sketch your life in three years on a piece of paper. Make vision boards if drawing isn't your thing. Visioning for a while may help you uncover your priorities and those of your spouse, if applicable, as well as open up new cerebral pathways and enable you to try on various life scenarios.

Accept experimentation

Prototyping, like any other design process, is a helpful tool to determine what functions well and what doesn't. Rent a property for two weeks and give relocation to a beach in Florida a trial if you're considering it. Go network with someone in that field and think about going on a two-week trip to a refugee camp if you want to help refugees. Joining a local writers' club is an excellent place to start if you want to create a great American book.

The lack of a clear strategy might cause anxiety in some individuals due to its unpredictability and ambiguity. If you are the kind of person who needs structure, I suggest choosing two or three focused areas to investigate, allocating a specified amount of time for this stage, and then making an activity schedule. Consider it this way: Developing these two or three particular interests or prospects is your new task.

If you're unsure of what to answer when someone asks what you do, simply list the two or three new topics you're researching as well as the work you've done in the past. Reluctant to part with business cards? That's OK. Printed business cards with your name and contact information are available; a work title is not required.

Establish a new goal and schedule.

Establishing routines is beneficial; one of my favorite proverbs is "structure sets you free." But without a reason to follow a schedule, it might be difficult to maintain one. (On the other hand, a routine devoid of intention is boring.)

However, after going through these changes, there's often a time when they haven't been used to their new routine or purpose. It may make you feel empty and make everyone around you a bit insane. This is typical. Having a persistent sense of boredom throughout a significant reinvention might be beneficial. Even if it seems forced at first, you will soon want to establish new habits and a sense of purpose for yourself.

I highly advise creating at least one new "identity" or interest area ahead of time if you have planning time before a change. For example, a legal partner I know is preparing for his impending retirement in two years by obtaining his mediation certificate. Another individual I know is getting in touch with a nearby institution to be considered to teach a course there.

These may or may not be successful, but they can provide some basic framework.

Charles, a longstanding mentor of mine, is a retired public relations professional who lives in Alaska and Washington, DC. I once heard Charles say that the life arc is learn-earn-serve. Charles, 66, believes that his current phase of life has meaning because of "archive activism." He established the Kameny Papers Projects, which is an archive of historical records related to Frank Kameny, the "Rosa Parks" of the LGBTQ+ community, in his words. Charles saw this emphasis as the result of his interests changing over time.

After a while, he accepted it.

You'll need motivation to get out of bed in the morning if you want to succeed in this next stage. Whatever it is, it must be in line with your beliefs and principles.

Make incremental progress in planning this next stage—not just financially but also as a person and a family. It's up to you to turn it into the most happy and fulfilled time of your life.

The Key Life Changes That Surviving Pandemic Lockdowns Can Teach Us

Many of us think that unanticipated shocks or incidents encourage significant changes in our lives and careers by causing us to reevaluate our objectives and goals. Regarding the coronavirus epidemic, it is accurate. In an online survey, I asked respondents how the epidemic had impacted their ambitions to change careers, and 49% of them said, "It has given me downtime to rest and/or think."

That's a great place to start, particularly for those of us who are reaching the end of our careers and are often too busy to think about the future. But if there's one thing I've learned over decades of researching successful job transitions, it's that thinking isn't nearly enough. Rarely do we behave in a new manner by thinking it through. Instead, we enact new ways of being and thinking.

Yes, there is a chance that situations that upend our daily patterns may spark significant change. They provide us with an opportunity to try out new pursuits and establish and maintain relationships. Even in the seemingly useless time, we spend away from our regular job life, we carry out significant inner labor, including answering the major existential issues, recalling our pleasant places, fortifying our will to make tough decisions, strengthening our sense of self, and more.

The epidemic brought about enough events for many of us to become acutely aware of what we no longer wanted. The issue is that there may not yet be more enticing, workable options. We are therefore caught between the old and the new. Furthermore, once the COVID limitations lift and we resume our usual lives and the workplace, we face a serious threat:

get drawn back into our previous careers and methods of operation.

How can people like us who want to change careers prevent that? How can we build on the lessons we learned during the lockdown to get closer to our objectives?

Studies on the transformational power of sparking events such as the coronavirus epidemic indicate that when we actively participate in a three-part cycle of transition—focusing on separation, liminality, and reintegration—we increase our chances of making long-lasting change. Let's take a closer look at each of those cycle components.

The advantages of divorce

John informed me, a businessman whose previous senior post ended at the start of the epidemic, that he spent lockdown in this beautiful, remote setting and was able to walk out into the country. He said, "I got to see the spring come and go." " I saw a lot of the natural world. It was just such a serene setting. My wife and I spent a lot of time together after we were married last year. I had been alienated from my son, and he came to live with us. That led to my getting to know him once again, which was wonderful. It was an extremely fortunate time.

John's encounter wasn't the only one. People who discover a new and different area to live in during the epidemic may have a higher chance of making life changes that stay, according to research on how relocating may encourage behavior change. 2. Why? due to a phenomenon referred to as "habit discontinuity." 3. When we are apart from the people and environments that bring up memories and past selves, we are all more adaptable. 4

Separation is usually the first step toward change. Separating individuals from everyone they knew before and denying them a foundation in their prior identities is a common operational procedure, even in some of the most extreme kinds of identity alteration, such as brainwashing, de-indoctrinating terrorists, or rehabilitating drug addicts. The reason for the transformation of young individuals upon moving away for education and the retirement of older persons from their careers may be traced back to this separation dynamic.

My most recent study has shown the extent to which "narcissistic and lazy" prejudice permeates our work networks. 5. The concept is this: We are naturally attracted to and stay in touch with individuals who are similar to us (we are narcissistic), and we get acquainted with and like close people by, making it easier for us to do so (we are lazy).

For most of us, the epidemic interrupted at least physical closeness. However, it may not be sufficient to lessen the strong parallels that our workplace's narcissistic and lazy biases cause. For this reason, at any point in our reinvention, it may be essential to keep some distance from the social circle that shaped our previous careers.

Researchers Tammy English of Washington University and Laura Carstensen of Stanford University discovered that people's networks shrank after the age of 60. This was due to people becoming more selective as they perceived their time as being limited, rather than because they had fewer opportunities to connect. Six It's likely that a lot of our pandemic experiences, similar to John's, will motivate us to reinvent ourselves by making us more selective about who and how we spend the little time we have.

Intrinsic Knowledge

Sophie was a former lawyer who was ending a two-decade career when the epidemic struck. She was interested in exploring a variety of new career options, including sustainability consultancy, nonexecutive board jobs, documentary filmmaking, and journalism. The period and space known as "betwixt and between" that was produced by the lockdown allowed Sophie to temporarily suspend the norms that regulated her professional life and explore a variety of work and leisure activities without having to commit to any of them. She made full use of that time, completing many courses, developing business concepts, working as a freelance consultant, joining a nonprofit board, and directing her first two short films.

By making the most of liminal spaces, we may try new and different activities with fresh and varied individuals. As a result, we have a unique opportunity to develop new connections, resources, skills, knowledge, and self-awareness. These digressions, however, are not permanent. Eventually, we must distill the lessons from our trials and use them to guide the next stages of our transformation initiatives. What merits are being pursued further? What recent area of interest is worth looking into? What will you give up now that you know it's not as tempting as you thought?

What do you only save for fun?

Upon assessing the situation, Sophie was taken aback to find that, while she had begun to form significant relationships with people in the film business very fast, she had not progressed as much in her board job as she had anticipated. She needed to acknowledge these things before moving on with the following phases of her transition plan.

Reintegration: An Opportunity for Fresh Starts

The majority of executives and professionals I have spoken with about their pandemic experiences say they are concerned about going back to their busy schedules and lengthy work hours, which take away from family time, even if they do not want to.

They should be concerned since it is unusual for exogenous shocks to result in long-lasting transformation. Usually, when we have a wake-up call of some kind, we just go back to our old habits as things go back to "normal." When Wharton professor Alexandra Michel looked at the long-term physical effects of excessive labor for four cohorts of investment bankers over 12 years, she came to that conclusion. 7. For many individuals, changing careers or even employment wasn't enough to prevent unhealthy work patterns. Even after switching to ostensibly less labor-intensive organizations, several of them had physical breakdowns. Why? Because, in reality, they had shifted into roles that were just as demanding, but they hadn't given themselves enough time to recover and separate psychologically from their tenacious selves in between roles.

Our actions within the brief window of opportunity that follows routine busting adjustments determine our capacity to benefit from habit disruption. According to research, for instance, there is a three-month window of opportunity after a relocation when one might adopt more ecologically friendly habits. 8 According to studies on the "fresh start" effect, people who return to work after a vacation have higher levels of goal-oriented motivation, but these levels peak on the first day back and quickly drop off after that. 9.

You must choose if the lessons you gained from the epidemic have a lasting impact on your career or whether you will just return to your previous position and routines as if nothing had occurred.

How to Design an Improved Retirement

How does a happy retirement feel and look? Everyone will have a different response, but financial preparation is only one aspect of a successful and seamless retirement transition. You need to make investments in your career and personal life in addition to your pension fund.

Job crafting, or customizing how you perform and think about your work, is a strong method to maximize your effect at work in the latter stages of your career, regardless of how long you want to stay in the workforce before retirement. It may assist you in developing the abilities, relationships, and experiences that will benefit you as you go on your next journey. In actuality, this entails figuring out how to use your interests and talents to mold your employment to fit your goals both now and down the road. As you prepare for a (literal) complete stop, this may include enhancing or decreasing elements of your work that you love or detest; seeking new possibilities; and adjusting or reducing your work obligations.

Amy Wrzesniewski and Jane Dutton, two scholars, are credited with coining the phrase "job crafting." 1. Researchers studying hospital housekeeping discovered that certain staff members went above and beyond the call of duty to actively customize their work. Since the first publication of their findings, several more studies have shown the effectiveness of job crafting for workers around the globe, from top executives to cooks. According to this research, intentionally adjusting our job may have a favorable impact on performance, well-being, and flourishing, as well as personal and professional development. 2.

Why Is Now, Just Before Retirement, the Best Time to Begin Customizing Your Work?

It may seem strange, but starting to create toward the end of your work may be a great idea. I have discovered that, in contrast to their younger professional selves, people in their later years of work often possess the confidence and credibility to shape their work and are more clear about what they want from their jobs and lives. This is based on my research and practice, which has involved helping hundreds of individuals and teams to job craft (as detailed in my book Personalization at Work).

A healthy "person-job fit," or harmony and alignment between our own needs and motivations and the work we perform, may be established and maintained via job design. 3. As our psychological, physical, and professional needs often alter in the latter phases of our careers, maintaining this fit might be especially crucial. For instance, we may not have as much energy (or patience) to devote to nighttime networking, or we could have parental care obligations to balance. Alternatively, we can be more interested in pursuing our hobbies or hoping to leave a good and long-lasting impression at work. We may mold our work to fit our changing and new demands by using job crafting.

Many unjust and antiquated beliefs exist around the disengagement of those nearing retirement from employment and personal growth. It can also be a prejudice we have against ourselves—if we plan to leave our job in five years, why learn a new platform or connect with new colleagues? Trying out different job creation strategies might act as a counterargument. It shows that you are not just coasting to the finish line, but that you are actively learning and evolving. In a proactive and good manner, job crafting may assist you in crossing things off your professional bucket list. It enables you to cultivate and preserve a development mindset, deliberately separate yourself from your job on your terms, and mitigate the sense of disconnection and distancing that many newly retired individuals experience. 4

You may also position yourself for success after retirement by taking part in job crafting. Job crafting might provide or enhance prospects for new employment since 70% of Americans want to work beyond retirement; side projects are not limited to individuals just starting their careers. 5.

How You Might Work on Creating Your Retirement Plans

Similar to individuals and their retirement strategies, job crafting takes many forms. Although work customization varies across individuals, there are five fundamental methods to utilize job-making in retirement: duties, skills, connections, well-being, and purpose.

Creating tasks

Task crafting is redefining the parameters of your work by introducing or eliminating tasks or adjusting things that you find enjoyable or irritating. You may optimize workflow procedures, systems, and meeting procedures by restructuring your daily schedule.

Consider Ian, a young, sixty-year-old structural engineer. He offered to chair selection panels and participate more actively in the company's graduate recruiting and internal promotion programs because he wanted to discover methods to support his organization's future. Although Ian used to oppose these kinds of things to put his client work—and, yes, his billable hours—first in his profession, he is now more driven to be a good corporate citizen. Ian can employ his technical expertise and knowledge in new ways thanks to the addition of these activities to his work. When he retires, he will feel more at ease and content since he has dedicated part of his time to advancing both himself and others' prosperity.

Expertise creation

The goal of skill crafting is personal development, which may include learning new things or expanding your expertise in certain fields.

Developing your financial planning abilities to help with retirement planning or pursuing specialized coaching and mentoring training are two examples of late-career skill creation. Advertising professional Brian began a blog to share his thoughts and forecasts on news and trends, hone his writing abilities, and position himself for success as a conference speaker when he retired.

Crafting for well-being

Creating a work environment that is more physically and mentally healthy is known as "well-being crafting." It's common knowledge that retirement enjoyment is significantly influenced by both physical and mental wellness, but developing healthy habits doesn't have to wait until retirement. Six

John, a university's chief information officer, voluntarily reduced his weekend work schedule to cultivate well-being. John recognized he needed to discover new methods to reenergize himself since he was on the verge of burnout. He'd tried, and failed, to just stop responding to emails on the weekends, but he was left feeling confused and uneasy. For John, the solution meant rekindling a previous love of photography. Taking up photographic challenges on Sunday mornings proved to be a more enjoyable and focused activity than responding to emails. Over time, he said he had less urge to check his email in the evening, even though he still permitted himself to do so. John had previously eyed local photography clubs that he was considering joining once he had more spare time since he understood that shooting pictures may positively impact the next stage of his life.

Relationship development

The process of building relationships at work entails molding our interactions with coworkers, clients, and consumers. This involves creating new connections, strengthening those that already exist, or combining and modifying existing connections.

As the chief people officer of a charity, Lisa cultivated contacts by participating more in local CIPD (the national HR professional organization of the United Kingdom) events. Her goal in expanding her network was twofold: first, she liked socializing with new people, and second, she believed this network would help her in her post-retirement endeavors of providing executive coaching to up-and-coming HR professionals.

Alice, who oversaw the customer care department of a bank, is another example. She said that she was purposefully limiting her contact, or trying her hardest to avoid, with certain coworkers she referred to as "mood hoovers"—people that drain your life. She informed me that "life was too short" to volunteer for causes or go to social gatherings with people she didn't like since she only had a few years left to work. (Alice, go!) When deciding which social groups, clubs, and committees to participate in more (or less) after retirement, this practical approach to relationships might come in handy.

Objective crafting

You may create a purpose by altering or reframing how you see components of your work that are important, purposeful, and consistent with your beliefs. You can also create a purpose by figuring out how to prioritize and cultivate areas of your work that contribute to your overall sense of purpose, both personally and professionally.

As a partner of a management consultancy, Jane was very committed to her client connections and found it difficult to think about handing up client accounts when she retired. She realized that the best approach to helping her customers going forward was to make a positive transfer, which was in line with her values, after carefully analyzing her purpose and actively rephrasing this action. She made a point of relishing the transfer, seeing transition meetings as a chance to think back on and remember the victories (and setbacks) she and her clients had experienced together.

A Workout to Assist in Creating Your Retirement

Job crafting is making room for yourself and finding the energy to be inquisitive about how you do your job and look for ways to make it better, similar to how an athlete works with a coach to analyze and refine their running form. Consider how, why, and when you do your task while answering these questions to help you reflect at work.

The exercises on the past, present, and future below might assist you in determining how to create a fulfilling retirement. You may jot down your responses, go through them with a friend or partner, or even illustrate and annotate your answers with drawings and sketches.

When doing this exercise, you don't need to have a particular job-crafting emphasis or type in mind. The first two steps will direct you toward a goal that will resonate with you and be relevant to you.

• The past Which aspects of your job have historically given you the greatest energy? Which accomplishments make you the happiest? Which criticisms have you treasured the most?

You'll get insight into the kinds of jobs you should pursue or hang onto as you approach retirement and beyond based on your responses to these questions. If you are a team player who thrives on using your skills and leadership abilities, for instance, you may want to look at post-retirement jobs that reward committee, trustee, or nonexecutive director responsibilities.

• The future When you retire, how do you want to feel? What excites you, in your opinion? In what way do you want to be remembered? At your retirement celebration, what do you want people to say about you? Which connections are you eager to break off, and which do you wish to keep?

This modified version of the classic future-work self-exercise, which is often used from the beginning of our professions, can assist you in defining a fulfilling retirement and guiding your present job in that direction. 7.

• Current. It's time to shape your present position to fit your future goals while clinging to your values.

The key to job-making is to begin small and approach it as a kind of lighthearted exploration. As a coach, I often assign people and groups to spend 10 minutes a day, or one hour a week, working to identify the tiniest and most beneficial ways to improve their present work by 1%. I advise individuals to choose the kind of work they create that most inspires and resonates with them at that particular moment, then look for a chance to engage in it.

One little skill-crafting experiment you could do would be to use an app to study Italian during the first ten minutes of your lunch break, in preparation for a long-planned trip after retirement. You could create a purpose by volunteering to get involved in something you care about at work, like mentoring upcoming leaders (within your organization or your wider professional field), or you could promote well-being by setting aside an hour once a week to go to the gym (and increase your chances of success by asking your team to keep you accountable).

A prosperous retirement is not something that occurs; it is something you create. When you approach a retirement job with curiosity and dedication, you may begin to turn your work around so that it becomes more fulfilling both now, when you log off for the last time, and in the future. As you enter this new stage, it may help you stay focused on the things that are important to you and give you a sense of control.

It's time to give your retirement plans some personality. You may position yourself for the retirement you want by designing the work you have now.

Retire with a goal in mind

Rufus Massey's career was rather active. His father constructed a two-room hut with rough boards by hand near Chickamauga, Georgia, where he was born. The phone did not work. The nearest neighbors were around 500 yards away. Life was never simple. However, the fortitude and tenacity he acquired as a young man contributed to his life's transformation. Rufus went on to have an incredible career in higher education and corporate America. He saw the development of technology in the telecommunications industry while working at Bell South. Before and during his corporate career, he worked as a student supporter and creative work program redesigner at Berry College, his alma mater.

Rufus decided it was time to leave full-time employment a few years ago. But he hasn't slowed down in life's speed. He performs in barbershop quartets and competes in singing contests around the nation. He enjoys playing pickleball and tennis, and he likes to hang out with his friends, family, and grandchildren. He goes back to his parents' old cottage to finish things up and take in the serenity of the North Georgia highlands. He dives for scuba divers. Some of the hundreds of students he has mentored over the years remain in contact with him, and he is now working on a book about his experiences. Though everything hasn't slowed down, Rufus's life has altered. "I enjoy challenges," he says to me. "I've always had a strong desire for adventure." And it's clear from this new stage of life. He has given up a fulfilling profession for an equally fulfilling, although more diversified, retirement.

At any age, we need to have meaning and purpose in our lives. The HBR Handbook on Developing Your Purpose states that I examine the notions that meaning is created, not discovered, that every individual has a variety of sources of meaning in their life and that these meanings change with time. Perhaps the most difficult transition to manage all those changes in meaning is giving up a full-time job permanently.

Organizing Your Transition with a Goal in Mind

Retirement is something that many of us anticipate and prepare for for years. After a lifetime of learning, working, taking care of kids, taking care of elderly parents, and generally feeling responsible for others, the shift might herald a new and exciting chapter in your life when you get to pursue your hobbies. When supported by sound financial planning, it may result in a brand-new level of independence. However, there might also be danger involved. For many of us, our connections at work are crucial, and loneliness and isolation are common problems for retirees. In a similar vein, work may provide structure, intellectual challenge, and purposeful objectives—all of which you should carefully consider replacing after you retire. And a lot of individuals experience a lack of direction after retirement. Even earlier retirement has been linked to early death, according to certain research; however, the reasons for this phenomenon are still up for dispute. 1.

Retirement is among life's most significant transitions, and transitions are inevitable. However, how can one effectively manage that shift, creating a purposeful existence after ending a career? I think that you create your mission rather than just falling into it. Furthermore, retirement is a unique and remarkable chance to start a completely new chapter in your life.

To do this successfully, you must first approach the shift proactively, making a mental note of what you are leaving behind and envisioning what you will replace it with. This kind of change is not unique to retirement. When we approach one of the several other life milestones—graduating from college, getting married or divorced, having children, losing a close friend or family member, changing jobs, or approaching another life milestone—similar things happen. However, accepting that change and handling it skillfully calls for a planned strategy. To successfully navigate this shift, follow these four fundamental steps:

1. Determine what is unchangeable. Finding the sources of permanency that give your life purpose is more crucial than ever in these times of change and uncertainty. You are more than your work, no matter who you are, and there are values that you should cling to that give your life meaning outside of the workplace. What do they consist of? Many people include their spouse, kids or grandkids, close friends, treasured pastimes, and religious convictions among them. To thrive in this new phase of life, it might be essential to recognize them ahead of time and learn how to depend on them.

2. Acquire the ability to release. Our jobs define each of us in different ways. This could apply

especially to those of us whose dispositions make it hard for them to truly disconnect for an extended holiday since they become immersed in whatever it is they do. Permanently letting go might be like losing a fundamental aspect of who we are. But you have to let go of the past to move into this new chapter of your life. When transferring control, be sure to do so completely and neatly. Give yourself enough time to establish clear boundaries between your new life and your previous one when you are quitting your job, at least initially.

3. hug people. Any time of development, upheaval, and transformation is made easier to go through when shared with others. Who will accompany you as you make the journey to retirement? A partner? A few close pals? a young person or an adult mentor? It will only seem clearer and easier to handle if you lean on these individuals throughout the shift, ask for their views, trust them with your ideas, and let them think through life with you. Tell the individuals you can trust about who they are and invite them along on the voyage. Furthermore, as connections and people are essential to happiness and purpose, just reaching out to others at this time of

change may give those interactions a fresh lease of life.

4. Dismiss inaction. It has been stated eloquently by Boris Groysberg and Robin Abrahams that you should never escape from something (like a job) without moving toward something else.2. That is valid even after retirement. Refuse to give in to temptation as you leave your work and the meaning it brought you.

to blindly transition onto the next stage. Rather, seize the chance to be ready for this new phase of life and whatever new meanings it may have.

That last element can be especially crucial for managing the transition to retirement. Individuals find meaning in many contexts outside of their professions, and when you take the necessary measures to enter a new and meaningful stage of your life, you will find it beneficial to delve into at least six timeless topics. Thoroughly considering these domains helps validate current areas of significance in which you can allocate resources and pinpoint new avenues for exploration. Love, avocations and self-improvement, beauty, occupation, religious or philosophical tradition, and service to others come to me when I conceive of them via the acronym LABORS.

adoration

The extent and quality of your good interactions are the most important factors in determining your level of happiness. 3. The risk of unintentionally being alone as you age is one of the main hazards. Strive to build a wide network of wholesome connections to proactively combat this. Leaving behind such professional contacts may be a challenging aspect of retirement. Retiring may, however, open up new opportunities for connections and strengthen the ones you currently have.

This will begin for many with family. One of the main reasons, even among those who like their jobs, is the chance to dedicate oneself to one's spouse, kids, and grandkids. It's a cliché, but spending time with family is vital to feeling useful.

Relationships don't have to end there, however. Like Rufus Massey, you have the chance to support and engage with people you formerly worked with, maybe even maintaining the mentoring connections you made along the way. Whether you choose to volunteer, exercise, or pick up a musical instrument, engaging in new activities gives you the chance to connect with others and create new relationships. Naturally, you could have pals who are approaching retirement age that you can go on trips with throughout life.

Interests and Personal Development

Giving up a full-time job might give you a lot more time to pursue your hobbies. Additionally, it may free up time for you to practice self-care, such as exercising, meditating, eating well, and pursuing your intellectual interests. These hobbies and self-improvement projects are a great way to find meaning in life at any age, but they become much more significant once you quit the workforce. It's important to keep in mind that retirement should be used to follow your passions rather than just as a means of getting "free time." Determining those pursuits and your goals as you get closer to retirement might also save you from feeling adrift.

Establish and stick to objectives in the areas of self-improvement—physical health, emotional health, and intellectual development—that you want to focus on during your newfound free time. Choose two or three passion projects or hobbies that you can devote time to in an organized manner, such as learning to paint with watercolors, making jewelry for craft fairs, or keeping bees. They shouldn't keep you as busy as your previous work, but they should give your days some structure and give you a feeling of challenge and achievement.

Grace

Beauty is one of the most difficult sources of purpose to discover in the middle of demanding work. I'm not referring to cosmetics or very gorgeous individuals, but those things can satisfy your criteria. Something that appeals to your senses, that is. Finding time to stop and enjoy moments of beauty may be challenging, whether you are working long hours at a desk or traveling for business. However, it has been shown that beauty and happiness are closely related and that beauty has the power to captivate, inspire, and challenge us, giving us a great sense of meaning and purpose. 4 Enjoy the great time that is retirement.

Which kinds of beauty appeal to you? How can you get the most out of it? Take a lengthy trek in the woods or a cross-country car trip to experience nature. Explore museums or consider learning to paint. Go back and read those wonderful, leisurely novels you've been meaning to. Additionally, enroll in the pottery class you've been eyeing. At every age, beauty is essential to a fulfilling existence, and retirement may provide more chances than any other period to enjoy beauty due to its independence and flexibility.

Employment

Of course, giving up full-time employment is the main goal of retirement. I believe that each retiree should question themselves about whether retirement really entails giving up work entirely or whether it should instead be seen as a shift to a stage of life in which work is just not the primary focus. I have seen several retirees effectively attain complete retirement freedom while enjoying the purposeful aspects of employment via part-time endeavors.

What part-time activities can provide you with some of the advantages of your previous employment, such as intellectual interests, professional challenges, and relationships? Maybe you've been wanting to write a book for a while. Perhaps you could use your years of knowledge to teach a class at a nearby institution. Alternatively, you may start a side business managing and purchasing rental properties or driving for a ride-sharing company to meet new people in the community. It's not necessary to completely give up work when one retires from full-time employment; one might just modify their job to better suit a new, more leisurely stage of life.

Traditions in Religion or Philosophy

Growing older is a time for introspection for most individuals. You are more aware of your mortality than ever before, having gathered a lifetime of knowledge and experience. Retirement may provide a great chance for those who haven't been very religious or philosophical in the past to reflect on the meaning of life and ask meaningful questions.

Approximately 85% of people on the planet identify as religious, and an even larger percentage follow some kind of moral and intellectual tradition. 5. Numerous studies have shown that religious adherents, especially those who participate in contemplative activities like prayer or community service, are generally happier, more involved in civic life, and even have better health results. Six Furthermore, both conventional and traditional knowledge warn us that "the unexamined life is not worth living." It's easy to get preoccupied with everyday tasks and ignore life's major concerns when things move at a fast pace. But retirement might provide you with the time and space to ponder these issues and find significance in the solutions you discover.

Use this chance to deepen your commitment to any existing religious or philosophical beliefs you may have. Participate in volunteer work at your synagogue, church, or other house of worship, or study religious texts with others. Spend some time exploring if you are unsure or in quest of something. Few individuals regret looking into life's deeper meaning, and many find that it offers an amazing source of satisfaction and grounding.

Assistance to Others

Nothing can change someone's life more dramatically than serving others. Serving others is fundamental to giving one's life meaning and purpose, according to several studies. 7. Additionally, studies have shown that volunteering reduces stress, fights depression, fosters happiness, boosts self-esteem, and even has a beneficial correlation with physical health. 8 It is a well-known fact that serving others makes us feel better, more satisfied, driven, and involved.

Whom can you retire to serve? Maybe you might volunteer as a mentor via a community organization or read at a nearby school. You may volunteer to clean up a park or help at a homeless shelter. You may volunteer more at your neighborhood mosque, sit on the board of the children's hospital in your community, or work for a local ballet company. Retirement need not be an entirely self-serving or pointless endeavor if you use your newfound leisure time and life experiences to help others.

A rudderless retirement can be avoided by planning to carefully navigate the transition to retirement by developing new sources of purpose through relationships, service to others, appreciating beauty, accepting life's big questions, and finding fulfilling hobbies or part-time work to use your talents.

Acquire improved transition skills

In my yard right now, a little, unkempt baby Robin is taking her first steps. Her gorgeous yellow hair is all messed up, and she seems a little lost and fatigued. I understand her feelings completely. Right now, she reminds me of several individuals I know. Everyone seems to be about to make a similar shift at almost every age: stepping out into an uncharted and unrecognizable new world.

I feel like I'm in the middle of being a baby bird and a great-grandmother, at just under 57. From this vantage point in the center, I can see my whole family perched on the brink of change, presumably engaged in a communal cliff ritual. Almost simultaneously and somewhat suddenly, we are all moving into our next chapters. My daughter is receiving her college degree. My kid is launching his first business. My spouse is getting used to what he doesn't want to call retirement. After receiving her first set of hearing aids, my mother has recently started moaning about the city's siren sounds. Not to mention my three wonderful friends—one who went abroad, one who lost her job, and one who ended her relationship with her partner.

All members of this multigenerational team are finding it difficult to let go of their past—their identities, communities, coworkers, and skills—to welcome their future, which is yet unidentified and unclear. There's uncertainty (time to move on), perplexity (what do I want?), and excitement (I am SO ready for a change) mixed with anxiety (who am I?).

We will experience these liminal periods more often as more people are enjoying longer, healthier lives. Thus, while I sit in the yard and watch Robin Jr. try out her newfound abilities, I'm also studying how to be ready for the decades that lie ahead. Regardless of our travels, we could all improve our ability to shift. Concentrate on five component talents to do this.

Timing and organizing

Because we are living longer, we must prepare for change now more than ever. Recognizing decades as a gift and determining what to do with them is necessary for making the most of them. Although it's often said that you can't have it all, time is a blessing that allows us to have much more than we ever would have imagined.

Analyze your life to date in terms of significant chapters. Adulthood was laid out by Erik Erikson at seven-year intervals. What were the high points, achievements, and lessons you learned throughout the last seven years?

Before you are 100, how many seven-year stretches do you have?

Make a timeline and position yourself on it from 0 to 100. This helps you gauge how far the road ahead could stretch.

Resigning politely

You can tell when an arc in a relationship, a career, or a life stage is coming to an end. When people live longer and experience more changes in their personal and professional lives, knowing when to end—and finishing well—will become an increasingly vital talent. Ends may originate within as a consequence of fatigue, sadness, boredom, or burnout. Alternatively, they may come from elsewhere—the land of reorganizations and layoffs, divorce, or other significant life changes. They serve as recreation's preface. Whether at work or home, it's not always an easy moment for everyone concerned. We may linger aimlessly for a considerable amount of time, pondering whether to remain or go. However, the finest foundation for excellent starts is a good finish.

You get agency when you make a choice. The first, and often largest, step is the decision itself, which is sometimes made years before you move.

Consider if you are remaining in your current situation out of fear or out of love. Do you cherish your current location, or do you dread moving on to uncharted territory? Though many of us are trapped here, the latter is a terrible place to live. Without this job, this pay, or this title, who would I be? Instead of being a terrifying question, it might be thrilling.

Accept uncertainty, ambiguity, and inquiries. Redefinition is found there.

And never forget that you are not alone while facing them.

Opening up from the inside out

One of the hard-earned benefits of growing older is self-awareness. Many of us don't explore our inner selves until the second part of adulthood. My friend Mary had always wanted to be creative, but she had never thought of herself as an artist until she started painting and writing when she was in her sixties. She is a published poet and a renowned artist at the age of 80. What aspect of yourself may be lurking in the wings, waiting? To get you started, here are some questions:

So far in your job, what have you found most enjoyable?

Which individuals and situations give you energy, and which ones make you feel depleted?

Do you wish to create yourself from scratch or transfer existing skills? Expand upon successes or forget about them forever?

In this phase, what type of balance will you prioritize? Concentrate on a single endeavor or build up a portfolio of side projects?

Should security be anchored or left up to the wind?

You should prepare a reassuring "travel bag" for this voyage, which may take many years: a financial strategy, a realistic timeframe, an advisory board of reliable supporters, and, if you have a spouse, explicitly agreed-upon assistance. It takes more than just upgrading your LinkedIn profile to be ready for the next thirty-three years of your life. As with any seven-year endeavor, invest in the following phase. Really?

Opening out to the external world

External input will be beneficial to any transition strategy. In essence, you're testing the market with your new strategy to see where you're most valued and required. Clare and Mark had assumed that, upon reaching their early sixties, they would retire, move out of their base in the United Kingdom, and settle in another nation. To discover the ideal location, the couple, who were in their forties, took a break from their jobs and spent three months each in four different nations.

Ultimately, this event influenced their decision to pursue a different career path rather than emigrate to another nation. To pursue their lifelong passions for sustainability and food, they decided to build an eco-friendly farm and relocate just one hour from their previous residence.

Herminia Ibarra, a lecturer at London Business School, refers to this process as "outsight"— traveling to these figurative new places to find not just what you love but also where you are liked. She argues that knowledge by itself may not be sufficient.

What qualities about you are most valued by others?

What is it that you have worked on or completed that gets the greatest praise, the most follow-up, or both?

Which of your experiments have prompted inquiries from individuals or projects that pique your interest?

When was the last time you felt alive, and where was it?

Springing forward

It is encouraging to see individuals who have effectively entered a new stage of their lives and made investments in causes close to their hearts— sometimes for the first time in their lives. Some individuals don't discover—or let themselves discover—their calling until they've satisfied every obligation they had to their families, parents, and previous expectations. Achieving ultimate alignment with oneself leads to a significant sense of liberation. The soul can never be fulfilled by wealth or fame. "The entire life of the individual is nothing but the process of giving birth to himself," as Erich Fromm said half a century ago. " We should be fully born when we die—although it is the tragic fate of most individuals to die before they are born."

Recalling that it's never too late to take flight might prove to be the true difficulty now that we have a few more decades to test our wings.

CHAPTER 3

Evaluate your choices and future directions

Arrange a Contented Retirement

After a lifetime of hard labor, you're almost ready to retire. The problem is that the things you have been looking forward to for years—lazy mornings, days spent tending to the garden, and visits to far-off places—don't seem like they will be sufficient to keep you going. A growing number of people are choosing encore careers—jobs that combine financial gain, a sense of purpose in life, and often a charitable component—instead of permanent retirement.

However, where do you even begin?

What professionals say

Nearly 9 million individuals in the United States between the ages of 44 and 70 are working in second-act occupations, according to Encore.org, a think tank that focuses on baby boomers, employment, and social purpose. "Because people are living longer and in better health, if you decide to leave full-time employment in your mid-60s, you have 20 to 30 years ahead of you. That's a long time," remarks Marc Freedman, the Big Shift author and CEO of Encore.org. "And then there is the existential question: Who are you going to be?" he adds, in addition to the financial one of how you'll sustain yourself.

On the one hand, thinking about starting a new job at this point in your life might be intimidating. However, Ron Ashkenas, a senior partner at Schaffer Consulting and an executive-in-residence at UC Berkeley's Haas School of Business, believes it's freeing to let go of the old and create a new identity based on "things that you find exciting, stimulating, or interesting." It's a chance to consider how you want to support your family, your neighborhood, and society. co-author of How Will You Measure Your Life? Karen Dillon concurs: "Leaving a full-time job doesn't necessarily mean that life gets easier," she asserts. However, if you're prepared to strive for your new objectives and keep yourself responsible, it might become more fulfilling. As you get ready for this next stage, consider the following:

Establish the foundation early.

Inform coworkers that you want to formally retire while you are still working if you are certain that your position won't be in danger. In addition to allowing them to determine if they have connections or a network they may use, Ashkenas adds, "Then it's not out of the blue." You must part ways with your employer amicably and let them know whether you're available for sporadic tasks and assignments, since this is a great opportunity to stay involved in your field. Dillon continues, "You can't simply stop working and hope that someone calls. Sow the seeds early, and opportunities and experiences will find you once you're in the market.

Take your time.

Give yourself some time, preferably many months, after leaving your employment to consider your future steps. Freedman advises, "Give yourself time to rest, renew, and restore." Handling this shift will take some time. You've probably been working and taking care of your family for a long time, so you haven't had much time to consider this next phase of your life. Understand that it may take two to three years to find a meaningful and gratifying job.

Consider this: What matters most?

Dillon advises making a list of everything that gives you emotional nourishment and then going deeper to determine precisely what it is about those items that motivates and brings you joy. You may, for example, mention working hard or spending time with your children, but you may also say, "What you most enjoy is having new experiences with your children, like travel." And working with others to create something is what you really like doing at work," Dillon adds. "Make time for the things that are important to you, and push yourself to make conscious decisions about how you spend your time." "Figure out what your priorities are at this juncture in your life," advises Freedman, which should be your aim.

Have an open mind to trying new things.

Freedman suggests adopting a "try-before-you-buy" mentality. He advises, "Find ways to dabble in things that interest you." Look for fellowships, internships, or part-time work; volunteer to serve on a nonprofit board; take on various professional projects; enroll in a community college course; or do all of the above. Dillon advises doing anything if it seems exciting, engaging, and like a way to learn new things. Seek methods to apply your well-earned knowledge to other fields as well, advises

Ashkenas. It's not as though your identity changes. You are adapting your abilities to new settings and circumstances, but you are still the same person.

Continue being productive.

Once you've taken some time off, it's critical to reintroduce some of the structure and camaraderie that office life provides. "You need things to look forward to and anticipate, just as you would look ahead to milestones in your work," says Ashkenas. Think about joining an online community, book club, freelancers' group, volunteer or religious organization, alumni association, or any other kind of group or community. You need the knowledge, banter, talk, and humor that come from a casual workplace setting, Dillon continues. Spending time with others who are "wrestling with the same challenges you are" is also beneficial, according to Freedman.

Make yourself responsible.

"You have to think about goals" while negotiating this shift, advises Dillon. "Ask the people who matter to you about how you're doing: your children, friends, spouse, or partner. Additionally, be open with yourself about your time management. Asking yourself, "Do I feel good and healthy?" can help you get a reality check. Do I sense arousal? Dillon advises against letting extraneous opinions influence your responses. Furthermore, Ashkenas advises that after determining your area of interest, you should constantly ask yourself, "Am I contributing value? Do I have something to contribute? Am I picking up any new skills?

Case Study: Use Your Skills and Network to Help Others

The earliest portion of Bill Haggett's career was dedicated to the shipbuilding industry. He held executive positions at Bath Iron Works in Maine and Irving Shipbuilding in New Brunswick, Canada. Bill felt compelled to give back to his community after moving back to Maine in the late 1990s after leaving Irving.

Constructing a new YMCA in his community is his top goal. Bill participated in the Y's fundraising efforts and the complex's architecture. "I come from a modest family, and I grew up in Bath, Maine, in the 1940s," he states. "The YMCA provided my friends and me with a great outlet."

The Y project was finished by the year 2000, but Bill had no intention of "going into retirement mode." He was contacted about a position by the Libra Foundation, a sizable nonprofit in Maine. They wanted to strategically invest in a potato firm that was close to going bankrupt in northern Maine. "Would I be willing to serve as chairman and CEO?" they inquired.

Bill had no prior experience in the potato industry and was not very interested in relocating to northern Maine. However, after considering his goals for the next phase of his life, he found the possibility to be interesting. "It was a way to boost the local economy by creating jobs and value in that area of the state," the man claims. Personal fulfillment would also come from the work. "I was drawn to the task of reviving this company. In addition to learning something new, I believed I could contribute some of my knowledge to the gathering.

Naturally, Potatoes had a difficult first years, but eventually, things got better: sales rose by 40%, and the firm made a profit again. It was acquired by California-based Basic America Foods (BAF) in 2005. Bill moved on to manage the meat industry in the meantime. However, Naturally, Potatoes did not live up to BAF's expectations, and Bill returned to the CEO position when a group headed by Libra purchased the firm back in 2010.

Bill, the chairman and CEO of Pineland Farms Natural Meats and Pineland Farms Potatoes, is eighty years old, and he has no intention of retiring. "It gives me energy," he declares. The fact that everyone I work with is younger than me is one of my favorite things about being my age. They are more tech-savvy, creative, and skilled than I am. It has been "stimulating" to learn a new business every few years, he claims. "I enjoy being of use and contributing."

How to Determine Your Dream Career After You "Grow Up"

"What's next?" I asked Sue Pfeffer, the superintendent of schools, on the eve of her retirement.

"I'm not sure," she said. "I'm still trying to figure out what I want to do with my life."

I became motionless. I was at a loss for words.

With a smile, she emphasized, "Life is a journey." That's the fun part of it.

I'm still developing. I have much to learn. When I pass away, I will cease. Travel? I told myself again. Pleasure?

I had doubts.

After all, I had met an investment banker not too long ago who began to question whether she was destined to be a banker after reaching the top. "I entered the finance industry because that's what people with business degrees from my school did," she acknowledged. Was it, however, truly what I wanted? I was ignorant of this.

I worked with a software developer at a tech business who began doubting himself after giving up on his startup and accepting "a real job." "I'm very content right now," he said. "I like the consistency. But for some reason, everyone is making me wonder whether I should be content.

I became even more perplexed when I ran across another person—a current college student who had just come back from their school's employment fair. They moaned, "My mentors keep telling me that I can do whatever I want."

"However, what would happen if I had a strong interest in both things at once?"

All of these people were struggling with what they wanted against what they wanted to do, what they could be doing versus what they should be doing, and who they were versus who they were. This was true regardless of their diverse professional phases and environments.

They're not alone; I'm confident, having conducted over 500 interviews with professionals across all career phases for my Wall Street Journal #1 book, The Unspoken Rules. Whether you're just starting in your profession or finishing off like Sue, you shouldn't let yourself get bogged down by big issues like these.

In the face of uncertainty, how can we achieve clarity? by seeing our professions as a lifetime adventure, much as Sue did? Your career starts with your first job and continues through your mid-career (and maybe other occupations), retirement (whether it exists or not), and beyond. A good trip also needs careful preparation, packing, steering, and reflection, just like any other. These techniques may assist you in managing the roadblocks that may arise at any point in your career, even if you cannot and do not know all that lies ahead.

Step 1: Conduct regular reflections

Assume you are traveling by car. Choosing the kind of vacation you're going on should be your priority before you even start driving. Some individuals want to get there as soon as possible because they have a certain destination in mind. Some don't mind if they miss one or two exits off the freeway. They can't wait to see the pictures, their friends, and the tales.

Asking yourself, "What matters more: the journey or the destination?" is a question that applies to professions and life in addition to road trips.

Are you aiming to achieve a certain role (like CEO), contribute to a certain cause (like climate change), assist a particular group (like refugees), achieve a certain lifestyle (like traveling the world, owning a certain type of car), or retire by a certain age when you consider your current career journey—or the path you'd like to explore next? If yes, you may be among the drivers who concentrate more on their goal while driving.

On the other hand, which of these things—work-life balance, meaningful employment, learning new things, collaborating with people you like, or financial security—do you value more? If so, you may be a driver who is more journey-focused and would want to concentrate on the road with one eye while taking in the passing landscape with the other.

It doesn't make you a bad person to want to work as a partner in a business law firm. It doesn't make you a lazy person just because you don't want to be one. It doesn't necessarily indicate indecision if you were a partner in a corporate law firm and don't want to be one anymore. You don't have to share the same objectives as everyone else. Also, your objectives don't have to remain constant. They definitely shouldn't, particularly as you close and open new life chapters. The most crucial thing is to understand why you're doing what you're doing right now. And when a specific voyage draws to a close, keep in mind that all journeys conclude with the prospect of new adventures. Thus, continue to contemplate. It's never too late, as Sue showed me.

Step 2: Make a thoughtful plan

When you launch your mapping app and place a pin, you'll see several potential routes and projected arrival times. Even if you eventually decide to forge your course, it is your responsibility to choose the path you want to take first.

Making plans for your profession and what occurs once it ends formally are not any different. Check out the biography, LinkedIn profile, or Wikipedia page of any person to get a general chronology of their life events leading up to this point. This study may help you see the patterns inherent in each professional route, the choices and sacrifices that lie ahead of you, and the places where you might wish to follow in the footsteps of others or forge your path forward—even if no profile is perfect and every profile has its embellishments.

Wikipedia, for instance, reveals that a lot of Hollywood actors waited years to be hired in a big-budget feature film before they were discovered for modeling or advertising. You can see on LinkedIn that a large number of private equity investors began their careers in investment banking rather than private equity. Podcasts and blogs will teach you that many entrepreneurs didn't jump ship and try their hand at side projects until they had enough traction and self-assurance to take their businesses full-time. Everybody begins and finishes somewhere, and there are trends in every field. An extra advantage of this study is that you will learn how other people handled retirement or a professional hiatus, whether it was by going back to school, taking a board position, volunteering, launching a company, relocating overseas, or any other means.

The next step is to seek assistance after you've determined which of the many pathways piques your interest. Make contact with a few others who've followed a similar route, give them a call, and pose inquiries like "I saw you switched from X to Y." How did you handle the changeover? "Given X and Y, what's your advice on what I should do next?" is another question you may pose. Although prejudices are a natural part of human nature, travel guides can only do so much. There's nothing better than asking a local for advice.

As you are studying and considering other options, remember to ask yourself, "Which path most interests me?" Make two lists of people who you consider to be your personal and professional role models as you examine others who have gone before you. Regarding your own life, think about the person whose life and ideals you would most want to follow. Regarding your career, think about the people whose efforts and accomplishments most motivate you. No one is flawless. Having a variety of role models allows for the complexity of life.

Step 3: Make a thoughtful packing list

Diverse tires and shoes are needed for diverse terrain. Different entrance visas are needed for different nations. You will, however, never regret bringing a toothbrush and extra underwear with you wherever you travel.

The same reasoning holds for managing every phase of your professional development: while certain career pathways may respect some qualifications more than others, all career tracks will offer you credit for the same credentials. Whichever route you take, whatever the road or weather conditions, you should always bring the same essentials: the capacity for effective communication and writing, interpersonal interaction, and rapid learning—skills that are likewise unlikely to be automated. So learn to feel at ease speaking, writing, and interacting with others. While you're at it, make it a practice to follow the news, particularly in the areas that pique your interest. Knowing what's going on and what's popular in their environment can help you communicate with more people and help you decide which possibilities to take advantage of.

Whatever career route you choose, you become a better salesman for your group, your concepts, and yourself the further up you go in a company. For example, if you begin working as a software engineer, "coding" is a verb you will likely hear used often. But by the time you become vice president of engineering, "selling" replaces "coding" as your everyday verb. You pitch ideas to executives to get resources, to your group to generate excitement, and to outsiders to draw in talent and, of course, generate business. Therefore, if your path includes receiving a promotion, be ready to keep improving and restocking your "pack," particularly in the area of sales.

Apart from the packing list that you won't regret, every route also expects you to bring extra supplies. Do you have an interest in data science? Stay current with analytical techniques. Do you want to work in marketing? Keep abreast of the most recent terminology, trends, and resources. Nobody will specifically advise you to hone these abilities and maintain them over time, but those who succeed—or remain relevant—will. You must thus unpack and repack as your trip continues, whether you decide to take on more work at work, take on a side project, or go back to school.

Step 4: Use Flexible Steering

Knowing when and how to change lanes—or maybe even get off the highway entirely—in the event of a flat tire, a road closure, an unforeseen desire, a health concern, or any combination of these—is essential to your whole trip.

Long-term career navigation involves avoiding job and industry changes, as well as managing your shifting interests and beliefs. Doing so may make the difference between feeling content and feeling trapped and unable to figure out why you are stuck. It's possible that your dream career won't even exist in ten years, just as your current work could not exist at all. In a similar vein, you may not desire the job you think you want in ten years. Various pathways may emphasize various talents, knowledge, networks, and certifications, which would further complicate the trip. It's not simple to switch lanes—just ask the academics who had to condense their 20-page CVs chock full of scholarly publications to a one-page résumé for industrial positions.

The secret is to recognize the patterns of the road and maneuver around them with agility.

The age-old chicken-and-egg dilemma, which states that you must have relevant experience to get relevant experience, is a crucial habit to break. Regardless of age or professional level, few individuals are prepared to give an untested person a chance. Such a "chicken and egg" situation often arises for young professionals, who must persuade an employer to give them a shot at that marketing position even if they have only ever worked in retail. For individuals who are later in their careers, it often entails having decades of experience yet still being deemed overqualified, too costly, or lacking the proper background. The hardest transitions are usually when you go from one industry or function to another (from sales at a pharmaceutical business to human resources at an insurance company, for example) since your new employer will find your past so alien. It won't be simple to change either the sector or the role (for instance, moving from pharmaceutical sales at one business to pharmaceutical sales at another). Modifying a single variable—the industry or function—remains difficult but manageable. Thus, pay attention to the variable that you are adjusting. Graduate schools, boot camps, and "returnships"—programs for people who took a professional break—may be helpful, but the success of your move will mostly rely on how well you prepare. When in doubt, use your expert internet research abilities to examine what graduates of your preferred curriculum get up to. You are moving in the correct direction if they are carrying out your strategy. If not, think about searching a wider area.

An additional significant motif is the well-worn proverb, "You have to see it to believe it." Trying a certain ice cream flavor is indeed the best way to determine if you'll like it or not, rather than spending more time analyzing your selections. Try it if you've already begun down a route and are debating whether to continue or if you haven't started yet and are paralyzed by analytical paralysis. Moving in any direction is the key to determining your direction, just as our map programs aren't very good at determining our orientation until we start walking. Thus, relocate— and begin gathering further data: Offer to help out with initiatives that go above and beyond your regular to-do list; ask to be introduced to someone you find interesting; and yes, think about taking up a side project. At worst, you'll discover things you don't like, and at best, you could find an alternative route that better suits your needs or advances you toward your objective.

A Ph.D. candidate who later became a real estate investor, Richard Zhang, once described to me the three stages of his professional path: Initially, he set out to fulfill his parents' expectations of success by putting in a lot of effort in the classroom, maintaining a high GPA, and pursuing a graduate degree in a subject he wasn't interested in as a vocation. Phase two was conforming to the social construct of success, which included quitting academia, going after a corporate position that had little to do with his education but was much sought after by his peers, and working himself to exhaustion. Phase three consisted of living up to his standards of success, which included quitting his corporate job, working out, maintaining a good diet, and finding a career that he was passionate about.

We're all trying to live up to our notions of success, and when I thought of Sue, who was wondering what would come next, the college student seeking guidance, the software engineer wanting fulfillment, and the investment banker seeking meaning, I realized this. We don't always have control over how our professions will develop or when certain phases of our journey will come to an end. However, no matter how long the journey takes or where it goes, thinking, organizing, packing, and guiding will help you enjoy it at any point in your career.

Dealing with an Unexpected Job Loss If you didn't have time to prepare, here's how to start healing

Over his more than two decades in the firm, Mike had successfully transformed failing departments into profitable, high-performing divisions. He saw a change in the organization's direction as well as a great deal of dishonesty, mistrust, and treachery when a new leadership group assumed control. Mike resisted cost-cutting measures that jeopardized quality and safety standards until he was informed that his services were no longer required.

Regretfully, Mike's experience is not exceptional. A person may experience a sudden loss of employment if they are fired or laid off if they feel forced to leave because they can no longer work for their company (because they witness unethical behavior there, for example), if they are transferred to a different position within the company, if they are called upon to take an early forced retirement, or if they are simply burned out and decide to leave.

Whatever the cause, losing a job suddenly may be quite upsetting. Mike put a lot of effort into his achievement and dedicated many decades of his professional life to this company. He had to cope with intense emotions such as rage, betrayal, loneliness, humiliation, and despair as a result of his heartbreaking loss.

Particularly when you've reached a certain position or income level, when you're responsible for household finances, when work has become an essential indicator of your moral worth, or when you feel like you've reached a point in your career or age where it would be difficult or impossible to start over, these emotions can feel intense, unwieldy, and even unmanageable. In addition, you could see that the forced change interferes with your routines, leads to unhealthy coping mechanisms, and seriously damages your connections with friends and family. If you have a spouse, those ties are severely strained.

You must get assistance throughout the agony to restore your mental clarity and your capacity to make wise, constructive decisions going forward. Take into consideration these suggestions to assist you in healing, staying whole throughout this process, and re-establishing your purpose.

Engage in self-compassion.

After a sudden job loss, you could have feelings of guilt or shame if you prioritized your well-being. You could be asking yourself, "What did I do to deserve this?" while you criticize yourself. What action might I have taken to stop it? However, this is the most unique opportunity to cultivate self-compassion.

First of all, acknowledge that this is one of the hardest periods of your life and that you should be especially kind to yourself. After that, put even more effort into getting back in touch with the individuals you care about outside of work. By spending quality time with them, you may de-stress, uplift your spirits, and strengthen your bonds with other people. By bravely discussing your thoughts with others and accepting their assistance and support, you may bravely allow yourself to be vulnerable.

Take care of your unfulfilled wants.

Using the SCARF model developed by neuroscientist David Rock as a framework, losing a job violates all five human social dimensions: relatedness (feeling safe with others), autonomy (feeling in control of events), certainty (ability to predict the future), and fairness (justice).1.

Losing a job is one of the most traumatic and stressful things that can happen to a person. If this resonates with you, don't downplay your feelings. Allow yourself time to process your loss and reflect on what you need to be healthy. Concentrate on restoring your physical and mental well-being.

Start by listing in your notebook the things you believe you have lost and the things you need to go on. Next, provide a list of things and people you're grateful for or anticipating. This will assist you in turning your attention from uncertainty and loss to control and onward motion.

Concentrate on the things you can manage.

Focus on the things you can control and use your emotional intelligence to manage your over- or under-reaction to the circumstances you find yourself in. It is ineffective to try to figure out why it occurred to you since it will only serve to keep you stuck in the past and slow down your progress.

Recognize the harsh reality you live in, but try to be positive and believe that you will overcome it soon. This shifts your focus from emotional self-control to problem-solving. Letting go and moving forward requires doing this.

Start small by using your talents and abilities for something like volunteering for a cause that matters to you. It will lessen your stress level, boost your sense of purpose, and assist you in regaining your confidence.

Recognize what you cannot change and be ready to move on.

Try to accept this shift and use it as an opportunity to grow, even though you didn't ask for it. Don't let your innate resistance to new prospects or possibilities become your barrier. Instead, use this time to reflect on the valuable lessons you learned from the job you just lost.

If you want to go that route with your job interviews, this will come in very handy. Putting up a good front for a recruiter or recruiting manager while you're mourning your previous position and afraid of being rejected again may be difficult.

Even if you have no control over how an interview turns out, you may utilize the knowledge you gained from your previous position to help you prepare compelling responses for your next interview. Your confidence will increase as a result, and your body language will show it.

Change your viewpoint and maintain an open mind.

By concentrating on your ideal self and the potential of the future, you may progressively transform your emotional reaction from one of loss and sadness to one of calmness, confidence, and control. Understand that it takes time, work, and purpose to go from shock and sadness to the optimism of new possibilities.

Make the forced change your gift.

Do I still have a job, or am I retiring now?

Should an unexpected business reorganization hasten your retirement plans, you may have to consider whether you're permanently out of the workforce. And you're undoubtedly debating some fairly significant issues, such as: "Am I retired now? Should I look for a new job? And if not, what awaits us?

Think about the following inquiries to aid in your decision-making as you ponder whether to remain retired or look into additional employment opportunities:

How do you see your days going, and how does work fit into your life?

What financial requirements do you have to meet your chosen lifestyle?

Who do you wish to use your abilities and talents to help or support?

How?

In this new stage of your life, what lessons do you want to acquire?

To feel your best, what do you need and desire from life and/or your job?

As you go and start to consider your options, be willing to consider accepting an "in-between" position—one that may not be in your preferred sector or one that pays less if you can manage it—and see it as a chance for professional development as opposed to a disappointment or a failure. Even though losing your job suddenly may be a very unpleasant and stressful period in your career, you can utilize this time to reflect on your life, reset your priorities, and reaffirm your ideals so that your choices will finally represent who you are and not the other way around.

It's easy to lose sight of the fact that you are an employee and that your work does not determine who you are. This is particularly true if you never really leave work and are always on. If you can distinguish between your work and your mission, you'll discover that a job is simply a job and that your purpose is a part of you that evolves and changes with time, just as you do. "Purpose is a process, not a state; an ever-unfinished accomplishment, not an algorithm," economist Umair Haque has argued. Give careful thought to not just your future course of action but also the people you want to assist with your

labor.

Following his unexpected layoff, Mike took some time to reflect on his values, the people he wanted to help, and how his profession fit into his bigger picture. His desired job was teaching, and he was able to get an adjunctship at a nearby institution. His pay went down, but his feeling of completeness unquestionably increased. When a full-time post opened up a year later, Mike took it.

He received the title of Professor of the Year three years later.

How to Use Your Retirement to Become a Coach or Consultant

Most older professionals are not interested in retiring. They would want to go on with their intriguing, rewarding work, but not at the fast-paced level of top corporate positions. That's why a lot of people are drawn to the concept of retiring from their "official" employment and going into consulting or coaching since it offers the possibility of flexible hours, better rates, and location flexibility. Naturally, there is increasing rivalry for these prestigious jobs. Globally, there are reportedly about 71,000 professional trainers, according to a 2020 survey, and 500,000 management consultants, according to the British newspaper The Independent.

In a field overloaded with elite colleagues, most coaches in North America are baby boomers. How can you stand out from the crowd? Here are five considerations to make if your goal is to work as a coach or consultant after retirement.

Give Yourself Enough Leap

Any change in profession causes some degree of disruption. You'll be better off the more time you allow yourself to plan and be ready (three to four years is preferable, but one to two years is okay). Albert DiBernardo, who is now leading strategy and development for a large engineering business, provided his board with a notice period of three years and specified his retirement date in his performance assessment. That was when he "cast my 'new beginning,' and it felt great," he recalled.

Giving your business enough time for succession planning enables you to make a considered exit and end your career with the knowledge that your legacy is in excellent hands, despite the worry of becoming a lame duck. Making your internal schedule will help you plan your money and any life adjustments (moving, selling your property, etc.) that your retirement and new employment may need, even if you would like not to disclose your plans to your coworkers so far in advance.

Perform a skills analysis.

You've most likely developed into an authority in your profession over time. However, besides subject-matter expertise, being an independent coach or consultant calls for a set of business skills. If you've allowed yourself enough time to prepare, you may use this to strengthen essential abilities like social media and public speaking.

You may also think about taking specialized classes to expand your expertise or going for a certification, but opinions on this vary greatly. 2. These might be university-offered executive education courses or professional programs covering everything from making online courses to becoming an acknowledged authority. 3.

Get to Work: Hiring Customers

Too many would-be coaches and consultants squander time, in the beginning, worrying about the operational specifics of their firm, such as the color of their logo. Until you have real customers, all of that is meaningless; therefore, getting them on board should be your first goal. While you're still working, take on a few volunteer clients in return for recommendations and testimonials to build experience as a coach or consultant (provided it's a positive experience).

You may have an edge over your younger colleagues as an experienced professional since you have built a network over decades that includes top executives who can recruit you.

NOT FIT FOR A COACHING ROLE? Attempt to instruct

If coaching or consulting doesn't seem like the perfect fit for you, a lot of CEOs consider teaching later in their careers as a way to give back to the community and find an intellectual challenge. I have been an executive education teacher for over ten years at business schools all over the globe, including Columbia University, Duke University's Fuqua School of Business, and prestigious B-schools in Brazil, Russia, Kazakhstan, France, Spain, and other countries.

Whether their objective is a side project on the side or a possible career transition into postretirement, here are three tactics business people may use to prepare themselves for an adjunct professorship.

Determine warm leads

Like with any job search, having an insider recommend you will greatly increase your chances of being noticed. Create a list of people you know who are employed by the colleges you want to contact, either full-time or part-time (LinkedIn may assist with this). Even shaky connections may be helpful if none can be found.

Get your pitch ready.

After determining who to speak with, you must prepare a brief pitch. At this point, avoid overwhelming readers with information; try to limit your message to no more than two paragraphs to avoid having them permanently put it on their "I'll read this later" list. A brief bio explaining why you would be a good fit to teach for their program should be included in the first paragraph. While academic achievements are certainly noteworthy and should be cited, your professional knowledge that is pertinent to this situation is more important. Citing any prior teaching expertise you have, whether it be from giving talks at conferences or organizing seminars for the organization internally, is also beneficial. Provide some suggestions for the kinds of programs or courses you may be able to teach in the second paragraph. Spend some time perusing their course catalog to get a feel for what they presently offer. You may recommend a combination of already-existing courses that you could teach and ones that you could design.

Prepare a resume and coursework in advance.

Your contact will request two things from you before the meeting if your query is answered positively. They will first ask for a curriculum vitae. CVs are a common format in academic settings and

are much more extensive than resumes, although they are comparable. Learn more about them. If you're creating the course from scratch, your contact will probably ask for the syllabus for the course you want to teach as your second item. Among other things, you'll need to outline the subjects you want to teach and the sequence in which you'll do so. The Higher Education Chronicle

Education provides a thorough manual for creating a syllabus. a

Teaching in graduate, college, or executive education programs may be a fulfilling experience that offers you the chance to learn new skills, take on new challenges, impart your well-earned knowledge, and get a useful new certification.

Start informing your current network of your future ambitions as your retirement date draws near, as they can end up being your first customers. After retiring, Roxann Kriete, who had been the CEO of an education organization and was featured in my book Reinventing You, did not promote her new consulting firm because she was inundated with more consulting work than she could take on.

Similar to this, DiBernardo started attracting potential customers by only telling his longstanding colleagues who are aware of his abilities about his goals, rather than using pushy sales techniques. "Some pretty senior professionals have told me they would hire me to coach them right away," he adds. Without my knowledge, they claim that I have done so for all these years.

Get Ready for Marketing

You may never need to advertise yourself since your current network might provide you with all the consulting work you'd want to take on, depending on how much of it you'd like to take on. However, if you need or choose to go beyond that, be sure you're concentrating on the appropriate topics. Some professionals devote endless hours to seemingly little details, such as choosing a catchy tagline or designing a business card. (If you can come up with something memorable, that's fantastic, but no coach or consultant requires one.)

Acknowledge the purpose of your marketing: creating a foundation of trustworthiness for when a prospective customer investigates you. To ensure that there is a sufficient quantity of information about your company online, concentrate on developing a professional-looking website with testimonials and a social media presence on at least one channel. You may, for example, start a blog on LinkedIn or another website for professionals.

Take some time for yourself.

Establishing a coaching or consulting practice might be daunting because of the expectation of doing everything at once. Start slowly, then. The majority of senior workers like to take their time transitioning into a new job; in a Merrill Lynch poll, 52% of participants said they took a sabbatical after officially retiring. 4 Even if you're not formally employed, you may use that time to quietly become ready, such as by honing your abilities and networking with potential customers, as previously said.

There are a lot of business-building tasks you may be pursuing while starting a new consulting enterprise, so it's easy to become sidetracked. Concentrate on doing the crucial things correctly: Whether you want to grow a steady company or just keep busy with a few side projects, know what abilities you can provide to your customers, use your network to identify them, and then promote just enough to draw in the correct amount of new business.

For retired professionals, coaching and consulting make excellent second jobs since they are fascinating, flexible, and often associated with high status. Although there is a lot of competition, by taking the above actions, you may set yourself up for a successful business that you can pursue for the rest of your life.

Are You Prepared to Take on Board Service?

Editor's note: Retirement may be a terrific opportunity to apply your knowledge, abilities, and experience to a charity or corporate board if your schedule and obligations during your working years prevent you from making time for board service.

To more accurately reflect the workforce and clientele of their companies, corporate boards are under growing pressure to diversify their membership. This includes hiring more women and minorities, as well as CEOs from a range of functional and cultural backgrounds. Simultaneously, the standard for "board readiness" has never been higher: directors are evaluated based on their comprehension of more intricate companies, technical proficiency, capacity to provide efficient governance, and ability to provide long-term, sustainable success.

What steps may leaders who want to be on the board take to set themselves up for success? How may someone get what's known as boardroom capital?

Regretfully, since you no longer have complete control over all the levers of operational authority, the skills required to sit around the top table, particularly in a non-executive role, are different from those that propel C-suite careers. For obvious contenders for the board, this is probably bad (but not horrible) news; they'll only need to put in the effort to acquire the necessary abilities. It's undoubtedly excellent news for nonobvious candidates or those who failed to make it into the ranks of senior management, who are still mostly male and predominantly of a particular race worldwide. They can begin on a more equal playing field, but they will still need to put in a lot of effort.

According to Laing O'Rourke, who has chaired three international companies in addition to the U.K.'s Institute of Directors, and Charlotte Valeur, a Danish-born former investment banker and non-executive director at The Bankers Investment Trust PLC, "We need to help new participants from underrepresented groups to develop the confidence of working on boards and to come to know that—while boardroom capital does take effort to build—this is not rocket science."

We spoke with over fifty board members from some of the top businesses in the world to get a deeper understanding of what makes a good director. Five key forms of intelligence—financial, strategic, relational, role, and cultural—are the foundation of boardroom capital, according to our research. You may not be surprised by the categories, but it is still vital to know why each one exists and to consider how you might do better in each one.

Five Categories of Financial Intelligence

Can you converse not just in words but also in numbers? Directors must be able to swiftly establish an educated view to carry out their fiduciary obligations.

the company's risk envelope, cash flow sustainability, financial gearing, or capital structure. The importance of these principles has risen in the aftermath of many crises involving audits and heightened regulatory scrutiny. However, conducting audits or holding a CFO position are not prerequisites for this duty. Crawford Gillies, a senior independent director on the Barclays board and a chair of many public and private organizations, states, "It's not a discussion about the technical aspects of accounting." "The ability to read an income statement and use it to understand what is happening in the business— what may be going well and not so well—is, in my opinion, the most important skill." Open up some old accounting textbooks, if you will. The ability to demonstrate that you are knowledgeable enough about the balance sheet to listen intently to a CFO, ask insightful queries, and hold them accountable if the financials aren't transparent enough is increasingly crucial.

Methodical

Proficiency in finance is one thing. Then, is it possible to convert them into strategy and vice versa? Director thinking should be guided by the following criteria, according to Ruth Cairnie, a former nonexecutive at Rolls-Royce and executive vice president of strategy and planning at Royal Dutch Shell. She is currently chair of Babcock and a member of the ABF board. Regarding the positioning and competitive advantage of our rivals, are we being truthful? Are the planned financials and the strategy connected realistically? After confirming that all the figures add up, the discussion moves to how the strategic whole may eventually equal a figure that is higher than the total of the accounting components. Environmental, social, and governance, or ESG, concerns are now of utmost importance and need understanding from any candidate seeking a position on a board. Our study revealed four distinct approaches by which directors have encouraged businesses to comprehend, express, and quantify sustainable value:

financial markets, or economies of capital

Experience (value propositions for customers and employees)

Mutuality (who and how you do business with)

Materiality (fulfilling your promises to provide)

Boardroom capital is the obligation to see a company's health, not its riches, as defined by Joseph Bower and Lynn Paine, rather than only its short-term value realization.1.

A quicker speed of change than boards have ever experienced is something you should be used to, as well as new business models and sector-specific strategies that are developing (be they services, software, technology, or digital, to mention a few recent examples). Some companies, such as the UK's Guardian Media Group, take great pride in their ability to dismantle and rebuild their strategic plans every 13 weeks. Fabiola Arredondo, a non-executive director at FINRA, Campbell Soup Company, Burberry, and Fair Isaac Corporation (FICO), notes, "Historically, boards would convene once a year for a strategic planning session." These days, I see boards more often incorporating strategic talks into regular board meetings and taking a deep dive once or twice a year.

ties

You have to step back before you can step up to the board. Not to operate but to examine support, and counsel is the job. You must establish fruitful working relationships with other directors, senior executives of the business, and other stakeholders, all of whom have unique backgrounds and viewpoints. Success in the boardroom depends on your ability to communicate effectively with others and, perhaps more crucially, to discern what others are attempting to say to you. Here, the stakes are high and the egos are big.

"One big team together, all from different nationalities, different places in the world, different backgrounds, working as a unit of people together and enjoying it," is how one of our respondents put it. However, as Valeur points out, it isn't always the case, and managing board relationships is important. To be productive, one must be able to listen intently, comprehend what is being said, process it, respond favorably, and swiftly modify one's perspective in response to recommendations made by peers that one may not have previously thought of. Coming from a less well-represented minority, she continues, "The one thing you need to be mindful of is that you are disrupting the boardroom by simply being who you are." Her recommendation is to maintain a varied voice while keeping an eye on the conduct of colleagues with more experience.

Function

Board members need to be explicit about what they bring to the discussion. One seasoned participant in the boardroom clarified, "We have eight meetings a year." Each board meeting is likely to give you the chance to ask one or two questions if you're fortunate. That's around ten inquiries a year, so you need to consider what qualifies as a substantial intervention. Consider why you were chosen for the board and what topics you can most effectively contribute to. However, Mike Clasper of Coats and previously Which? Limited points out that the tough aspect of being a non-executive director is not figuring out when to ask the same question again or pursuing an underperformance problem in the first place.

Cultural

"To create an environment where the executives feel willing to be forthcoming, to admit if something is not going so well, and to seek the board's advice and guidance on how to fix it," is the responsibility of the board chair and other members, according to Mary Jo Jacobi, a former senior corporate executive, senior U.S. presidential adviser, and current board member of The Weir Group and Savannah Resources Plc. When that isn't always the case, it is wrong to create an atmosphere where executives must be seen as successful, and moral, and that everything is going well.

In these endeavors, any director may support their board chair. This degree of openness, trust, and rapport is the result of meticulous planning and coordination, the capacity to assess a group's culture rapidly, identify areas for development, and create a strategy for enlisting supporters and gradually guiding the organization toward change. Because of improper dynamics and chemistry, Ruth Cairnie cautions, "I have experienced plenty of organizations where you have very capable people but don't get anything like the best out of them."

Developing Those Capabilities

Our knowledgeable group advises that you don't need to be flawless before starting a boardroom job. However, if one of your goals is to become a business director, you should start accumulating board-relevant expertise as soon as possible.

Here are several methods to begin:

Financial: Take ownership of your P&L if you haven't already; pay close attention to how assets, investments, and leverage work together to create free cash flows; and watch and listen to earnings calls online.

Strategic: Get more familiarity with the business model of your company and learn how it links to your operations and strategy, as well as how changes might create, release, or jeopardize economic value.

Relational: Look for chances to speak with and report to your board, and follow up on possible positions where you may make decisions at the head of internal departments or in other capacities. Observe and take notes from people you deem knowledgeable. Make sure you facilitate others' success, both inside and outside of your team.

Role: Pay attention to the role you have been assigned and the areas in which you are most valuable. In all of your meetings and tasks, you may put this into practice. Respect those who approach their jobs and relationships with the same level of accuracy.

Cultural: Join cross-functional, cross-industry, and cross-cultural groups to hone your ability to read, get along with, and enhance the culture of varied sets of peers.

Considering the kind of board member you want to be also helps. In our research, we identified four typical strategies (this is not an entire list; there are still more variants and combinations, such as the potential for board members to assume various responsibilities at different times):

Police like the more and more regulatory role that board members must play; the finest ones hold CEOs accountable without adding unnecessary burdens of rules and paperwork.

Data addicts are target-oriented, highly skilled, and financially literate, but they should refrain from asking for too much information and behaving too logically when interacting with executives and colleagues.

Successful architects understand the delicate balance, structure, and flexibility of short-term profits and longer-term fiduciary and custodial obligations. They seek to build solid foundations that will last beyond their board tenure.

From 30,000 feet, pilots can see everything. They understand and can explain how value is produced, improved, safeguarded, and provided; yet, they must use caution to guarantee successful takeoffs and landings.

Lastly, we would strongly advise you to communicate your desire, goal, and potential to lead at this level to knowledgeable colleagues and connections. The information you present on your resume should vary from what you have used before when sharing it. Rather, you should demonstrate your potential by listing your strengths in each of the five intellectual domains.

The Retirement Handbook for Leaders

Simon, a CEO in the media, stated, "I'm not quite sure what to do next." Before turning 30, Simon worked as a CFO and served as a top executive for fifteen years. He had tripled earnings and quintupled income at both public and private businesses. But Simon was thinking about retiring after his business was just sold. He hadn't had time to think about retiring, as many CEOs and executives do, since he was too busy managing the business.

More than 100 CEOs of S&P 1000 businesses retire annually. Preparing the current CEO for the next stage of their career is a crucial component that is almost always absent from succession plans, even from the smoothest operating systems. According to Scott Davis, the former CEO of UPS, "I was so focused on the CEO job, I didn't spend time figuring out what I would do next." The CEO of Johnson & Johnson until recently, Bill Weldon, agrees with most CEOs when they say, "I didn't do a lot of thinking about post-employment while I was still the CEO." I then exited the off-ramp at 110 mph and rapidly reached zero. Retirement seemed like a void.

CEOs often retire in their early sixties, which is still considered reasonably youthful by today's standards. Few people must work to make a livelihood. Still, the majority want to work, and they do. Thirteen of the fifty top executives in the Fortune 500 were interviewed, and their post-CEO careers were examined. Nobody went to the golf course to retire.

Almost all of these past CEOs made contributions to the American economy and the welfare of society, even if very few went on to hold additional CEO positions. Among them, almost 25%—all former CEOs of Fortune 500 companies—became involved in private equity. More than half took on leadership roles in nonprofit institutions, and almost all of them were charitable. Serving on public boards was two-thirds.

Numerous people have authored books and lectured.

Leaders who retire have to deal with a loss of enormous responsibility, status, and influence. It does seem like you may have gone down the elevator shaft over the first several days, as former Northrop Grumman CEO Ron Sugar put it to us.

It may be particularly difficult for women. Former Xerox CEO Anne Mulcahy cautions, "Retired women CEOs have a special place in hell." When you reach retirement age, your children have also left the house. Retirement is doubled over.

"The things that work for you as CEO work against you as a retiree, such as being in charge and your high energy level," Mulcahy adds in her warning. She claims that it took some time for her to get her bearings—"calendar filling." But not for long, as she found employment that gave her meaning and enthusiasm as chair of Save the Children, lead director of Johnson & Johnson, and guest professor at Harvard. "It wasn't about money or visibility for me; it was about impact and utility."

Any emotion of loss that comes on suddenly is fleeting. After becoming CEO, almost all of the CEOs we spoke with expressed a tremendous deal of pleasure in their jobs. They were relieved to be free of the business schedule, even though they were very proud of their work achievements.

After retirement, CEOs and other leaders find great value in themselves. Dick Parsons, a former Time Warner CEO and head of Citigroup says, "It was almost surprising to me how much you have to contribute." But you quickly come to the realization, "I can help here; I've seen this movie before."

"It was unexpected how rapidly I was presented with the opportunity," concurs Doug Hodge, the former CEO of PIMCO. "A few weeks after I retired, I received interesting offers from venture capitalists to get involved with fintech startups and to join a prominent board. I've given myself a reset.

So how can leaders rise to the occasion and achieve success in their second stage? Like Simon, the majority of CEOs we met with were too busy operating their businesses to think about retiring. We found some guidance in our study to help retiring CEOs and other executives prepare for Act II.

Arrange your off-ramp.

Former American Express CEO Ken Chenault counsels executives to prepare their exit strategy while they are still employed by "identifying the categories of things that are important to them," rather than just by focusing on "specific opportunities." Without a strategy, leaders run the danger of "falling into the abyss," cautions Chenault. Spend some time organizing your priorities. Don't disregard it. It is crucial to exercise thoughtfulness. Chenault advises considering one's familial, charitable, and commercial interests. For instance, Chenault was aware that he intended to concentrate on digital and technology in his company job. Chenault states, "In this way, I was ready because I had thought about them," when possibilities presented themselves. Chenault was able to act swiftly and decisively at the start of his off-ramp because he recognized what was essential to him, even if he was unsure of precisely what he would do.

Give it some time.

The most frequent mistake is accepting invitations too soon in an attempt to fill the emptiness. Say no to everything that is given to you for the first six months, as Ron Sugar advises. The majority of the time, you shouldn't accept the first offers you get. CEOs consistently informed us that moving too quickly was the one thing they truly did wrong, necessitating the unraveling of agreements. One CEO, for instance, agreed to join the board but had to resign shortly thereafter to take a better, more prominent position. It would have made more sense to go slowly. Say "yes" gently and "no" frequently.

Get ready to take care of yourself.

Even the most confident leaders may find themselves in a strange situation of self-doubt and self-questioning after retirement. According to one CEO, "It prepares you for dealing with yourself." Mulcahy advises, "You need to know who you are when you're done being CEO." "That entails reflecting on aspects of your personality and temperament and occasionally modifying some CEO traits," the speaker continues. Upon hearing that Parsons was a writer and teacher, his wife asked, "And what will you do next week?" He needed some time to discover his passion. He questioned himself about what his childhood dreams had been. He founded a jazz club since he had always wanted to own one. With the thought, "In the worst case, I could drink the results," he also purchased a vineyard. "There I am in the soil; it's a product; there is dirt under your fingernails; it's tangible," he exclaims, clearly loving it. This is quite intimate. "What are the things you will enjoy?" is a question Bill Weldon of Johnson & Johnson suggests asking yourself.

Join forces with your spouse.

To translate a business phrase into a family setting, you and your significant other must have the same expectations. If your partner has been waiting patiently and now wants to travel, and you want to return to work, this is the perfect opportunity to create a family-approved, or at least mutually understood, shared plan. We spoke with CEOs who both intended and increased their family time. Ken Chenault and his spouse set aside time for meaningful pursuits together.

Take up the position of mentor.

One sense of loss is particularly difficult for leaders to get over. The power is not the issue. It's the populace. Scott Davis said, "The people," which many others repeated when asked what he missed most about his profession. Through the years, I made a lot of friends that you don't see as often. By seizing the chance to mentor others, leaders may bridge this knowledge gap and get immense satisfaction from sharing their knowledge. We have encountered things that other people have not, as Bill Weldon once said to us. We may use the lessons learned to assist others. The former CEO of ADM, Pat Woertz, is an advisor to a Chicago business accelerator and serves on the boards of P&G, 3M, and Northwestern Hospital. In addition, she is "saying yes to more people than I was able to before" by mentoring other women.

Make a time-allocation plan.

Put your desired number of hours per day and days per year on paper. As Ron Sugar points out, we should provide "surge capacity" since a variety of engaging activities might sometimes result in unforeseen time needs. Scheduling no specified time enabled Dick Parsons to take over as Citigroup's head at the most dangerous point in the bank's history during the financial crisis. Afterward, Parsons took over as the team's manager at the NBA's request when the Los Angeles Clippers' original owner was chastised and fired for making racial statements.

Spend equal amounts of attention on for-profit and nonprofit endeavors. Choose the areas where you want to contribute and where you wish to earn money. Lastly, make a note of how much time you want to dedicate to personal interests or family time. "The beauty is you can try things out you haven't been able to before," remarks former Pfizer CEO Jeff Kindler. He then poses the question, "What are the things in your professional life you never got around to?"

Return the favor.

Not many former CEOs refer to their new phase of life as "retirement." Contributing to society is the most common topic we hear. Dick Parsons' statement that "we owe back to our society" encapsulated the feelings of many previous leaders. We are required to back the platform. After retirement, Parsons led the Rockefeller

Foundation and established two acclaimed eateries with an African-inspired menu to help resuscitate New York City's Harlem neighborhood via jazz music.

"The philanthropic side of retirement provides psychic reward and payback far better than any money we receive in our for-profit work," as Bill Weldon puts it best. Now is the ideal moment to lay the groundwork and start allocating your riches. Every CEO we spoke with has a giving heart. Ken Chenault, for instance, is a member of the Harvard Corporation and serves as head of the board of the Smithsonian's Museum of African American History. Ron Sugar is a national trustee of the Boys and Girls Clubs of America, a member of the board of visitors at the UCLA Anderson School of Management, a director of the Los Angeles Philharmonic Association, a trustee of the University of Southern California, and a director of the World Affairs Council of Los Angeles. Scott Davis is a member of the Carter Center Board of Councilors and a trustee of the Annie E. Casey Foundation. Together, the 13 former CEOs we spoke with for this piece are on at least 25 charity boards.

Leaders can navigate one of the most difficult decisions of their career with this guidance: leaving.

Additionally, the prospects are enormous, as Jeff Kindler informed us. Having had the chance to see what retirement life would be like before retiring would have allowed me to organize my preparations in a matter of months as opposed to years.

CHAPTER 4

Make Decisions

Selecting a Significant Alteration

Individuals have several reasons for making significant professional changes, such as switching employers, launching new businesses, or quitting their jobs entirely. For others, the epidemic proved that flexible and remote employment was feasible. Others were encouraged to reassess their priorities as a result, especially about striking a balance between their personal and professional lives. Additionally, for some people, the virus was accompanied by a big flashing "YOLO" sign that encouraged them to overcome their anxieties and pursue their lifelong goals.

These three instances demonstrate the significant impact the pandemic had on our way of thinking about our profession, although they are by no means all-inclusive. While we shouldn't discount the lessons learned from the epidemic, we should also make an effort to avoid being caught in a one-way door by pressing these realizations against some of our most blatant prejudices.

Reasons to Exercise Caution

Our judgment is not flawless. We never experience a completely logical process as we would want to, partly due to the imperfect knowledge we have at our disposal, as Nobel winner Herbert Simon showed us. Additionally, Amos Tversky and Daniel Kahneman noted that our judgments are further biased by our own psyche.1. Unfortunately, during periods of change, these elements greatly influence people's thoughts.

I recently had conversations with two managers who were trying to go forward in the same company. Jason said that he was more productive at home and that he would want to go to a job that permitted more remote work. As the sole team member present at her location, Helen, on the other hand, felt alone, disengaged, and out of the loop. (Every name has been altered.)

Both Jason and Helen concentrated on elements of their work environments that were very vivid and conspicuous for them in this "grass is greener" scenario. Both of them needed to take some time to consider the big picture and balance the advantages and disadvantages of each setting. Very few decisions to shift jobs will be beneficial or terrible on their own; every move has costs and advantages. Even if it's challenging, to see things more objectively, we must leave our local settings.

The extraordinary experiences we've had throughout the epidemic are having an impact on our mentality, which is making matters much more challenging. Data indicates a strong connection between the epidemic and mental health deterioration, which may seriously affect one's ability to make decisions. 2. Chris, a manager, told me it was time to step down and hunt for a new position. He confided in me that he didn't see a career path that attracted him and that he felt disconnected and uninspired in his present position. After additional conversation, it became clear that Chris was more worried about his general mental health than his employment at the moment. He was among the vast majority of workers whose mental health has deteriorated since the epidemic started. 3. In his specific situation, talking to his family made him realize he was mistaking the source of his unhappiness and that the solutions he was thinking about would not significantly fill the void in his life; in fact, leaving his current organization would mean leaving behind a network of support he had grown to rely on.

Take the following actions to ensure that you are approaching your decision-making carefully and considering ways to lower your own risk before making a significant—and perhaps irreversible—career choice.

Boost the decision-making process

To start, think about ways to enhance the information (and interpretation) that goes into your choice so that the result is more precise.

To improve your chances of identifying psychological biases when they occur, start by briefly brushing up on some of the more prevalent ones. 4 Even after more than 20 years of teaching about biases, biases such as the following still influence my decision-making:

Anchoring: The propensity for judgments and approximations to be impacted by an initial benchmark, or "anchor," such as the asking price of a vehicle or house.

Confirming evidence is the tendency to prefer information that supports our preexisting beliefs. Examples of this include recognizing and accepting news reports that support our opinions.

Availability: The tendency to overvalue information that is easier to recall due to its freshness, vividness, or emotional intensity. Sales of lottery tickets, for instance, often rise after the announcement of a large victory.

Framing: The idea that the way a choice is presented has a significant impact on our decisions For instance, we often move more quickly to prevent a loss than to realize a gain.

These and other factors are influencing our approach to making the important professional choices we are discussing.

"Outsource what you're bad at" is one of my favorite maxims; in this instance, that's staying objective. Discuss your choice (and its limitations) with those you know will question your presumptions and, in turn, dispel your prejudices. This is an example of outsourcing to others. Devil's advocacy is nothing new and may even seem obvious, but especially in trying times, we have a tendency to withdraw into the security of talking about our opinions with those who we know feel the same way. Seek out someone impartial towards your final choice, and tell them that they can only be of assistance if they are honest with you.

Put some framework around the decision-making process to outsource it. Making career choices involves a great deal of complexity and significant risks; it is almost hard to remain objective when addressing them head-on in their totality. Rather, use a methodical technique to dismantle and outwit them. 5. For instance, make a schedule of how you will assess each factor in your choice and allot a certain amount of time for each before you begin to consider it. This guarantees that you will neither overlook any part of the equation nor devote excessive or insufficient attention to it.

It's crucial to establish your procedure before beginning to consider your options. In this manner, you may prevent unintentionally altering your procedure in a manner that confirms your prejudices.

Boost the Quality of Decisions

Next, think about how to better carry out your choice to lower the possibility that it will turn out poorly.

Sometimes, even with the finest of facts and procedures, we all come to a less-than-ideal decision. These mistakes may be especially expensive in the wake of the Great Recession.

Recall that you are in charge of your risk management, so take some time to consider ways to lessen your exposure if your choice proves to be unwise.

Applying the Jeff Bezos and Sir Richard Branson-favored method of dividing choices into one-way and two-way door decisions is one way to do this. Six choices that are reasonably simple to reverse are known as two-way door choices. Bezos and Branson both contend that rather than spending a great deal of time considering and arguing about these choices, we should just test them out and then reverse them if necessary. Decisions involving the two-way door provide excellent learning chances. One-way door choices, on the other hand, are hard to change, if not impossible; therefore, it is worthwhile to take the time and make the effort to thoroughly study and weigh all of your alternatives before deciding on a course of action.

First and foremost, you should consider whether making the job shift you're thinking about is a one-way or two-way option. Perhaps you've desired to take on a new position in your present company or launch a side venture. You're in luck if you believe the change you're thinking about will be reasonably simple to stop or reverse. Give it a go and see what you discover.

If that's not the case, however, and you believe that the expenses make the door one-way, consider if there is a method to change that choice to become a two-way door. As an often-cited example, during the Virgin Atlantic launch, Sir Richard Branson secured a provision in his contract with Boeing that permitted him to return the aircraft he purchased if the airline failed to take off. Although he avoided having to employ that condition in the end, by negotiating it, he changed the decision from being a one-way door to a two-way door.

Is there a way, in the framework of your present company or employment, to accomplish a comparable set of professional objectives? Could you go on a hiatus or work fewer hours to test things out or get more information? Can you expand or fortify your relationships and professional network to broaden your alternatives if your planned course of action does not pan out as you had hoped?

Understand that the one-way/two-way door difference is only a heuristic; deciding whether something is one- or two-way is a personal choice based on your risk tolerance and financial constraints. What one individual deems too expensive to reverse could be reasonable for another.

Remember that you may convert a one-way door choice to a two-way door decision without spending any money on an "undo" button. Recall that a one-way door choice is essentially one made because you believe the consequences of failing would be too great to bear. Making the choice eventually two-way also means lowering your vulnerability to an irreversible decision. Therefore, if you are unable to reverse your one-way door decision, consider if there are any methods to reduce the cost of a poor choice. You've effectively made it a two-way door choice if you can make the cost low enough that you're ready to bear it if things don't work out and you decide to walk away.

Talk to each other.

Many of these suggestions call for an honest and open discussion about your present job, which may be risky and frightening. Recall that if your present employer loves you, they will want to assist you in resolving any doubts you may have and collaborate with you to negotiate a fair settlement; the alternative is a letter of resignation that offers little opportunity for a win-win arrangement. Observing 20 years of MBA candidates through the hiring process has taught me a few things, one of which is that we often undervalue our capacity to express our demands, bargain, and reach a reasonable compromise. Although there is no assurance, finding out how much your company values your well-being is valuable information in and of itself and is pertinent to the whole process.

Everyone was greatly affected by the epidemic, and many people had to reassess their priorities and come to some important realizations. These are legitimate and significant, and they shouldn't be disregarded. But we're also all humans, and as such, a variety of things impact how we think and make judgments. Acknowledging and deliberately tackling these prejudices throughout pivotal life choices are crucial measures in ensuring we don't end up trapped on the wrong side of a one-way door.

Emotions Don't prevent people from making wise decisions

I once spoke at Cornell University as the keynote speaker on how to make sure our choices are more successful. To start, I surveyed the approximately 2,000 attendees to find out whether they were concerned about making a mistake when faced with a significant choice. A staggering 92% of participants said "yes."

I then asked the audience to list the kinds of errors they were afraid they would make in one or two words. A word cloud created from the most popular answers revealed that many of us are concerned that we depend too much on instinct or our gut. Members of the audience were particularly concerned about moving too rapidly, acting hurriedly, impulsively, or impetuously, and making snap choices.

Given the widespread concern that hasty judgments lead to blunders, why do we make them?

Tough and complicated emotions are usually experienced when presented with tough and complex choices. Many of us want to rush the decision-making process because we don't want to deal with these painful emotions. However, this often results in bad choices. We often feel worse off in the end and may not fix the current issue. It's a counterproductive feedback cycle that leaves us feeling bad about the choices we make.

However, you may use these emotional bookends as a hidden weapon to help you make wiser judgments. It's as easy as taking the time to recognize (1) the feelings you experience when confronted with your choice, and (2) the feelings you want to experience when you glance back at your choice. What do you observe? How is your life better now that you have made a satisfactory decision?

This four-step exercise helps us avoid making reactionary decisions by training our cognitive, or "wizard brain," to monitor and control our emotional, or "lizard brain." This is how it works.

1. Determine which choice you must make.

In addition to our emotions, we often have to filter through a lot of contradicting facts while attempting to solve a difficult issue. Determine what choice you need to make as a first step.

Consider Charlie as an example. While pursuing his doctorate, he developed a technique that enhances hearing. He is currently the CEO of a neuroscience business and is very dedicated and informed about all aspects related to his innovation. However, he lacks experience in business, and he must make several crucial decisions: To get his product on the market, how can he effectively use the money he has already raised? What is a realistic amount of money to invest in creating and testing a minimum viable product? How can he get more funding for his new business?

Charlie's backers want him to complete his clinical research and develop a product for pilot program testing. He feels that he has a very limited schedule, and he wants to fulfill it and do the right thing for his investors.

Charlie has been advised to locate a business-savvy partner by a few of his advisors and investors. Charlie must decide whether he wants to enlist the assistance of a cofounder with a background in business to assist him in solving these issues.

2. Determine your feelings about the choice you must make.

As you consider making a significant choice, think about your feelings. Which emotion is prevailing in your mind right now? Is fear the cause? Fear? A feeling of being overpowered, or maybe enthusiasm about the prospect ahead? Do your emotions stem from past encounters or further sources of knowledge?

Naming our emotions may aid in establishing a little emotional buffer between our sentiments and our behavior. By gaining that distance, we can analyze the emotion and recognize that we are experiencing it without allowing it to take the place of conscious cognition and agency in our decision-making.

Charlie is a firm believer in his invention and wants to see others benefit from this amazing technology. He doesn't know how to make the choice and feels trapped. Regarding his other stakeholders, he is apprehensive and nervous. Investors and advisors are giving him mixed messages; some are certain that he should bring on a business-minded partner, while others maintain that he can do it alone if he can learn to manage his time more efficiently.

For Charlie, establishing the space to acknowledge that he felt trapped was revolutionary. It made him understand that he was the only one who could make decisions as the CEO and that he wasn't trapped at all. He also understood that the term "stuck" wasn't appropriate. Rather, he reported feeling reluctance. He was able to do further analysis when I explained to him that resistance is a psychological response rather than an emotion. In reality, he said, he was uncomfortable. The explanation opened my eyes. He might investigate his uneasiness now.

3. Show off your accomplishments and feelings.

Let's say that you've made a wise choice. What is your current state of mind? Do you feel relieved or like you've accomplished something? Do you now know where you want to go with your life? Have you improved your connections or advanced your career?

Charlie discovers that the unease he has when considering hiring a cofounder is due to concerns about potential conflicts arising from having to share decision-making authority with another person. Though, in the end, he doesn't want to share ownership of the project he has dreamt of and toiled over for so many years, he did not feel confident in the expertise of the person he recruited. Even though his uneasiness had been present the whole time, it took him a while to realize it.

4. Use the poignant bookends.

After analyzing your first choice and the emotional justifications behind it, ask yourself the following question: Have you accurately defined the choice you are making?

Charlie applies emotional bookending and discovers that he has confused many options, which is why he feels knotted up. It wasn't about whether or not to bring on a cofounder; rather, it was about whether or not he wanted to share ownership of his company. He had thought that, like many of the companies around him, he would need to bring on a partner to acquire the necessary commercial skills.

However, the emotional bookending activity made it clear to him that there were alternative approaches to obtaining the business acumen required by the organization. He might appoint a consultant or someone who works under him. While the relationship is a long-term commitment, the business decision is just temporary. He hadn't considered the long-term effects of having a companion, in addition to confusing the options.

We believe we don't have enough time to devote to the decision-making process, and we most certainly don't want to linger in the uncomfortable emotional states that significant choices evoke, including worry and annoyance. It might be simpler to let our emotions and lizard brain take control while making difficult choices.

Although it seems magical, calling upon our wizard brain is not magic. To see the lizard, we must put in the effort to slow down, identify our feelings, and sit with them. Using our wizard brain allows us to work with our emotions instead of letting them rule us.

To better identify—and make—the true choice, the one that will enable you to go into your future with clarity and confidence, emotional bookending helps you recognize and accept your feelings rather than hiding or avoid.

CHAPTER 5.

Retirement Is Difficult- Don't Try It Alone

Establish Your Board of Directors for Retirement

For you, what does retirement mean? to put in less work? regain more command over your time? to at least pick up the Italian language? To do a voyage across the Pacific Ocean aboard a sailing vessel Do you laugh because you can't see yourself ever wanting or being able to afford to retire? Or do you intend to work until you are unable to do so in some capacity?

We are aware that retiring after 40 years with the same employer and gold watch is no longer the same as it once was. What is it now, though? It involves collecting retirement income or benefits and determining what to do next for a lot of us. There are many, many different possibilities, and maybe too many possibilities. It's comparable to the free-form decision you made upon receiving your university degree. Me? Who am I? What kind of life do I wish to lead? Where would I want to reside? If you were fortunate enough at the time, you probably had a support system of mentors and decision-makers who trusted in your skills and talents. An informal board of directors to guide you through your retirement choices is just what you need right now.

Why create a board for retirement planning?

Throughout your career, you have undoubtedly had both official and informal mentors, particularly at the beginning or throughout significant professional transitions—people you spoke with before choosing to accept a new position or seek assistance in resolving an issue at work. You may have slowed down your networking efforts as you get closer to the end of your working career and see retirement as a one-person show. But working with someone else to prepare for your retirement is preferable. Putting together a group of people you can turn to for guidance, support, and ideas can help you plan a happy and rewarding retirement.

It takes conscious effort to build an unofficial board of directors for your retirement. The sole need for membership is an agreement to support you as you consider retirement, test concepts, make decisions, and adjust to your new reality. Meetings are not necessary.

You should be straightforward and subtle when asking for assistance; for example, you may say, "I'm researching retirement options." I value your viewpoint. Could I sometimes run some ideas past you?

Here are some people to add to your retirement planning board after you have your objectives in mind and your questions ready.

The officials

Whatever path you choose to take when thinking about cutting down or ceasing employment entirely, there are four types of individuals you should have on your board of directors.

close relatives and friends

Those who will be most affected by your retirement decisions—friends and family, for the most part—should be the first individuals you include on your retirement planning board. Likely, you've already begun discussing retiring with your close friends and relatives. Your spouse is an obvious candidate for your board if you have one, but there may be other people you care about, such as your parents and adult children.

monetary counselor(s)

Getting trustworthy financial advice is necessary when quitting a consistent source of income. If you are employed by a major corporation, schedule a meeting with the benefits representative. Schedule a meeting with your financial advisor as well, if you have one. To create a retirement plan, if you don't already have one, get advice from an impartial financial adviser. These professionals can assist you in determining when to retire as well as how much money you will have in retirement.

Health advisor(s)

There are health issues associated with this period of life, so you should include people on your retirement planning board who can assist you in understanding your choices for health insurance. Any financial advisor can assist you in determining the kind of health insurance you need, whether or not you should join Medicare at the time of your move if it is a possibility, and what kind of private supplements you may need to add to the national health insurance program in your country. However, you should schedule a health examination and discuss any changes you may need to make to your diet or exercise regimen after retirement with your primary care physician.

legal counsel

Finally, if you are leaving a family company or partnership, you should think about adding a lawyer for a will, a healthcare proxy, or any other legal guidance.

These four fundamental members of your board of directors—close friends and family, your financial and/or health adviser(s), and an attorney—are the individuals you should keep in touch with as you make more and more retirement-related decisions.

The experts

Your decision over which course to take will influence how you decide to expand your retirement board of directors beyond the executives. You should add individuals from the new areas you're considering to get a sense of what that choice is like, as well as people who know you and can help you throughout your search, such as existing mentors or coworkers. This is true whether your retirement is volunteering or spending more time engaging in a passion project, whether it involves working fewer hours and taking on a smaller position at new employment. Speak with professionals in the industry you are pursuing to test your theories. You will need a mix of "from" and "to" members on your board, even if the former are venture capitalists and the latter are potters. These are some suggestions for structuring your board and soliciting feedback, depending on your retirement plan.

Giving up your job abruptly Incorporate past coworkers.

Some choose to play golf and suddenly retire. The temptation therefore becomes to neglect your professional network and include a golf pro on your board of directors. However, you need to wait a year or two to hedge your bets. After a year or two, some individuals get bored in the absence of more scheduled activities. Therefore, if you have retirement guilt and want to look for something new, maintain two or three individuals from your working life on your board of directors for a few years. They know you and what you are excellent at. This way, you don't start from scratch.

Making a move to a new area or career? Identify fresh mentors.

Some flip the page by leaving their former profession behind and starting a new one, rather than quitting entirely. An accomplished sales and marketing professional loved her vacation home and the neighborhood, and she believed that working as a real estate agent there would be a fantastic way to augment her retirement income. She made connections to real estate companies there and pitched herself to one whose CEO helped her get her license and get off to a solid start. She added two close friends from the area to her board of directors, along with the CEO, and this helped her establish a stronger bond with the year-round community.

Applying this realtor's strategy to your situation would be as follows: determine whether you need to increase your retirement income, identify a passion project that you can use to generate that income, and include on your board members from both your new endeavor and your former employment that can attest to your abilities.

Going easy on retirement? Take your manager with you.

The head of graphics and communications for a charity involved in media decided to ease into retirement. He convinced management to provide him with a three-month contract to finish a significant project after he retired. That marked the beginning of his modest consulting business. In addition to adding two colleagues from different media companies and a member of a relevant professional society, he also added his boss as a reference to his informal board of directors. He could take on fewer assignments and increase or decrease his consulting hours since he had a strong board of directors and was in charge of his schedule. At first, he set aside July for a family trip every year. Finally, eight years later, he decided to take a full retirement.

Consider your professional talents to get an idea of how you might ease into retirement. Are there any special abilities you like to use? Could you volunteer or sell them to a different employer? Are you a recruiter for corporations? You may work as a headhunter. Do you have a CFO pension? Consider promoting your abilities and background to other businesses in your sector. If you think this route is possible for you, consider including representatives from professional services businesses on your board of directors.

How to Put Together a Board If You're Not Sure What to Do Next

It's time to review your options if, like many others, you put off thinking about retirement because you're not sure what you want to do, when is the best time to retire, or even whether you can afford to retire. They can provide you with the basic knowledge required to assist you in finding the answers to your inquiries. You don't have to make a decision right away if you are content with your employment, but if you are becoming more cynical and feeling stuck in your organization or position, you should think about retiring as a way to leave behind the things that are causing you distress.

Indeed, initially, deciding on a retirement strategy will resemble the feeling of "now what?" you most likely had after graduating from college. However, you have changed since then. You now possess a reputation, abilities, contacts, and experience that you lacked back then. Find the ideal individuals for your board of directors by using your contacts and colleagues. They can also assist you in exploring your alternatives and, if you have a choice, in making an informed decision.

For instance, a well-known marketing executive gave himself a year to decide what he wanted to do when he retired since he hadn't given retirement any thought while he was still employed. It was suggested by his unofficial board of directors that he take a vacation to unwind. His visit to Australia's Great Barrier Reef piqued his interest in climate change. He assisted his daughter's climate change NGO in honing its message back home. He connected with state lawmakers via his board of directors and appointed one of them to the position. He discovered his new career path as a climate change activist in less than a year.

Pay attention to your future.

When you were a first-year college student, do you recall realizing that you were no longer the powerful senior in high school? Retirement can seem abruptly demotivating. Some retirees never fully let go of their pre-retirement status and instead focus on the past.

You must look ahead if you want to retire successfully. Saying something like "I was the COO of a tech company" or "I was an executive in human resources" draws attention to the past. It will be difficult to find chances, find individuals who can help you shape your destiny, and appoint members to your board of directors.

Even if you haven't made up your mind about what you want to accomplish yet, make a statement about who you are going ahead. It will be much simpler to introduce yourself to new people, grow your board of directors, and change the way you see yourself if you have an "I am" statement.

Here are a few instances of "I am" utterances with an eye toward the future:

"As a retired logistics manager, I am seeking a chance to contribute to a company such as yours."

"I'm a former CEO hoping to join the board of a nonprofit in the field of education."

"I'm retired and trying to get better at golf."

Put your best "I am..." statement on and adjust it till it fits. If it isn't comfy, adjust it. Put potentialities in writing. Get some practice with your board of directors and pals. Or make a few "I am..." declarations for various situations. After you've successfully transitioned into your ideal retirement, you'll be able to proudly declare, "I work as a real estate agent in one of the most picturesque towns in the United States." Alternatively, "I provide design and communications consulting to media companies." Alternatively, "I love that my family and friends come to visit me because I live in a seaside community."

Creating your board of directors will assist you in the process, no matter how you define retirement. After you have successfully adjusted to retirement, serve on the board of directors of another person as a way to give back.

Your Retirement and Your Relationships

Your retirement is undoubtedly yours, but it's not yours exclusively. It is also, in sometimes deep ways, your partner's, your family's, and your friends'. When you leave your working days behind, you encounter a tremendous transition in life that affects the people closest to you, and you are also impacted by them. Retirement will bring about a lot of changes in your life, such as how you spend your time, how your days are organized, who you are in groups, and how you interact with others. Relationships may be the most significant of all of these; prior studies have shown that relationships have a significant role in a person's retirement well-being, including emotional and cognitive functioning as well as physical health. 1. Additionally, sustaining some of your current connections and forming new ones might help you adapt to retirement more easily, enhancing your later years with happiness and support, according to a recent study that my colleagues and I have been doing.

In this chapter, real-world examples from my team's eight years of study are used to provide coping tactics and thought-provoking questions. In addition to other data collection methods, we have conducted repeated interviews with 14 individuals throughout their retirement transitions to get as much insight as possible into their social and psychological experiences. 2. Through long-term follow-up and one-time interviews with an additional 69 older adults (some recently retired, some still working), we were able to dig deeply into relationship dynamics and how retirement can affect relationships both positively and negatively. We also looked at what retirees can do to make their relationships better. 3.

Think about Jay and Debra, who had quite different ideas about what they wanted out of retirement. Over more than six years, I conducted ten interviews with Jay, a management consultant, as he neared retirement, entered retirement, and experienced the early years of his retirement. In addition to continuing the many social and charity activities she had been involved with before they became empty nesters, Debra wanted to spend more time alone with Jay. In contrast, he yearned to rekindle his childhood enthusiasm for hot rods, spending many hours by himself in his workshop modifying the recently purchased vehicle and discovering the nearby hot rod club. In the first year after retirement, these differences led to many misunderstandings, hurt feelings, and arguments. For instance, there were times when Jay was deeply involved in intricate metalworking and Debra wanted to go on a romantic picnic, or when he was settling in to watch a favorite TV show just as she was getting ready to set up lunch in the den for her book group. They enrolled in couples therapy after realizing they needed assistance navigating their relationship during this difficult period. They finally reached some of the happiest moments of their marriage by finding compromises that required patience, dedication, and hard work. They gave each other space and time each week while also rediscovering each other when they took road trips throughout the nation. Nonetheless, conflicting notions of what retirement should entail and the frustrations these notions caused one another never really went away.

Simon's experience as a spouse was significantly different. He couldn't have been more ready to retire with his second wife, Helen, who just resigned from her position as a nutritionist. However, he had to continue working for two more years to meet his alimony obligations. They jumped into retirement life from the day he eventually took a break, becoming closer via long morning talks, tending to a garden together, and volunteering for political issues they were enthusiastic about. Simon and his spouse went through a very simple and seamless adjustment in their married life.

The most reserved person we've been following, Margaret, had been widowed for several years before. She planned to cherish her time with Trudy, who had been her closest friend for many years, and maybe even meet some new acquaintances. Even though she was wary of social situations and worried about every encounter, she eventually discovered that retirement allowed her the emotional space and time to form a few friendships that would enrich her life and be mutually beneficial, all while strengthening her bond with Trudy.

Retirement relationship dynamics

As you approach retirement, the story of your relationships with your spouse, family, and friends might not be as challenging as Jay's, but it also won't be as easy as Simon's; rather, it will probably fall somewhere in the middle, with a mixture of hardships and joys, much like Margaret's. Your actions before, during, and beyond retirement will have a significant impact. Though there are many things you can do to mold your connections to fit comfortably, you can't control everything regarding the quantity and quality of your relationships in retirement. Of course, what fits you comfortably will vary depending on your personality and goals for retirement. These may include finding meaning and purpose in your activities, having a steady stream of enjoyable days, weeks, months, and years (you define "enjoyable"), rejuvenation and relaxation, self-discovery, meaningful connections with others, learning, and development, or something entirely else. Determining that will be a terrific place to start when considering constructively how your relationships may support or interfere with your ability to realize your aspirations.

Your accomplice

Include the person you spend the most time with in your life, if there is one, in your retirement narrative from the start. Before choosing a retirement date, the great majority of individuals we spoke with spoke with their partners about the financial elements of retirement. To our surprise, however, a surprising number of them stopped there and didn't elaborate on what their real life will be like—day to day, month to month—after retirement. We have a suspicion that Jay and Debra's post-retirement relationship would have started much better and much sooner if Jay had been honest with both of them about his intention to spend a large portion of his time on hot rod activities. When the time for their joint plan for daily life together finally arrived, Simon and Helen had those conversations and worked together to develop a few specific ideas about how to spend their time during that first postretirement year. Their plan was flexible enough to accommodate unforeseen opportunities and challenges.

It is hard to exaggerate how crucial it is to have a detailed conversation with your spouse about what your daily retirement will entail—at the very least, a few possibilities that both of you find appealing—so you can adjust to uncontrollable circumstances. At this point, the story of Lawrence and Cynthia is instructive. In a very broad sense, they did plan their retirement together. They developed their retirement goal of relocating to a far-off state where their son and his wife resided to assist in caring for their cherished toddler grandson a few days a week. Sadly, they hadn't thought about what to do or what other connections they would need in their life except for that little family when they weren't with their grandson and his parents. They didn't even get to know their neighbors after relocating; they didn't make any friends or participate in any clubs or activities in their new neighborhood. Their son's marriage broke down the year after their relocation, drastically reducing their contact with the grandson, and as a result, their problem drinking turned into a severe alcohol addiction. Cynthia and Lawrence were able to restore their health, salvage their marriage, and finally build a joyful retirement full of wholesome connections only when they enrolled in a long-term residential treatment facility after their third postretirement year and continued to participate in a 12-step program. In hindsight, Lawrence said that they might have more successfully weathered the storm that life brought at them if they had formed the habit of discussing the specifics of their everyday lives and had strategies for fostering community early on.

If one of you plans to retire before the other, think about how your lives will function, on a very detailed level, in the interval. 4 Who is going to cook, clean, and do errands around the house? Before his retirement, Simon and Helen had decided that she would handle the majority of the job, after which they would split up the household duties. Before her husband's retirement, Irene retired in her mid-60s, and she accepted the duty of managing the conversion of their vacation cottage into their permanent residence. Indeed, while her husband was still working, she enjoyed having the freedom to personalize that area and carve out a niche for herself in their new neighborhood. Nonetheless, one or both of them may have been resentful if they had not already reached this mutual agreement.

Your household

Members of your extended family and your adult children will be impacted by your retirement, and vice versa. By proactively considering what you want those connections to become, you can influence that effect. Helen had never really been welcomed by Simon's daughter, who had two little children and resided in a different state. Before retiring, he would never see his daughter without going alone, out of consideration for her sentiments. Nevertheless, he informed his daughter rather softly but strongly that from now on he would either see Helen or not at all, as he realized he wanted his marriage to be the focal point of his life after retirement. When his daughter gave in, Helen quickly became close and affectionate with her stepdaughter's whole family.

Jay didn't talk much about his adult son before he retired, calling their connection good but distant due to his son's hectic schedule. However, Jay was thrilled to see that his kid shared his renewed enthusiasm for hot cars. Together, they went on road trips and became closer. When Debra suddenly passed away during a routine operation, their link kept them both steadfast; while they grieved, father and son found solace in one another.

Retirement may also be a significant time to reconnect with distant relatives, so think carefully about which ones you might wish to maintain. Douglas, who had been raised abroad, yearned to spend more time in retirement interacting with his distant extended family. In their first year after retirement, he and his wife organized several trips, with rest pauses at home in between. Because of this, he was able to restore some of those relatives' connections with one another and strengthen others that had previously only been maintained online.

Your companions

Retirement offers chances to find new pleasures and comfort in both old and new acquaintances. Margaret sought out connections via new activities after reading that relationships are essential to aging well and realizing that she would have to overcome her inclination to spend her days curled up with her dogs and books on the couch at home. She immediately formed a small but lively group of friends via lessons at her neighborhood gym and participation in a weekly spirituality group, with whom she found tremendous delight and, subsequently, considerable support when her health started to falter.

Irene had made a lot of solid friends with her neighbors and coworkers at work, and she anticipated that she would maintain those relationships after moving into the summer cottage. She was surprised to find, however, that those friendships soured in the first few months of her retirement and that it was okay to part ways with them now that she shared fewer interests. To her surprise, regular walks in her new neighborhood and the art lessons she had enrolled in to follow a long-held interest naturally brought her new people, some of whom she later became good friends with.

How to Discuss and Contemplate Your Retirement

What does all this have to do with your retirement? It implies that as you approach and navigate your retirement years, you will need to give serious thought to your most important connections.

You might begin thinking about how you might want to alter your relationships by asking yourself the following questions: After giving them some thought, talk about them with the individuals who matter most in your life, if appropriate:

In terms of your most compelling identities, characteristics, inclinations, and driving forces, who are you at this point in your life? When you retire, who do you want to be?

What expectations, anxieties, ambitions, and objectives do you have for your retirement years?

Are there any connections that you want to keep or grow to help you achieve your goals, given who you are, who you want to be, and what you want out of retired life? How may you do this—by spending time together in person, communicating virtually, or doing both at once? Do you have any relationships you'd want to end? Do you want to take others in a different direction? Think about the pleasant, casual connections you need and the deep, personal relationships you may require in the future, as well as the concrete support and assistance you need to provide and receive.

Do you feel that you need to make a change in your life by becoming involved in new activities that might lead to new relationships? If so, how? Think about your neighbors and other group members (like churchgoers), particularly the retirees. What social events might you attend again or establish to meet potential new friends? If you click, start by chatting after church or the club meeting and arranging to go out to eat or take a stroll together. Develop a "yes-day" mindset, as one retired person puts it, even if you're an introvert. Maybe even more so. Simply accept an invitation from someone you admire if it doesn't require a significant time commitment, such as attending a book reading or bocce club. It may bring about a new friendship.

How well-defined are your plans for your days during the first months and years after retirement, and how well-aligned are they with those of your spouse and other significant individuals involved?

Regarding your retirement, what expectations do the important people in your life have, and what do you have of them? When you retire, would your spouse, who is still employed, expect you to take care of everything around the house? Have you spoken about your requirements and preferences for daily routines, spending time together vs. apart, labor division, and utilizing the areas in your house while you're both there if you're retiring at the same time? Do you have retirement plans that don't align with your partner's desire to travel the globe or your daughter's expectations that you will be able to care for the grandchildren?

What are the ramifications for the significant others in your life if you want to make a significant post-retirement move, such as relocating to a different community? Additionally, what can you and they do if the adjustment proves to be less successful than anticipated? Can you (and they) jointly imagine appealing options?

Kindly ask yourself and the people in your life these kinds of questions to think about and debate, keeping in mind that you and they will both be influencing each other's relationships. Think about how you will respond in those relationships—both anticipated and unanticipated—while being true to who you are and what you need in retirement. Our study demonstrates that you may avoid some unpleasant retirement traps and get some of its finest rewards by approaching your relationships with awareness and purpose.

It Can Be Stressful to Retire

Retirement is a dream come true for many of us. When we first start working, we often don't give it any more attention than filing taxes or signing up for a savings account. We fantasize about it, laugh about it, and sometimes even worry about retirement age as it approaches. Will we be fortunate enough to spend our elderly years with health, wealth, and the company of loved ones? For those whose whole existence has revolved around their career, the shift to not working may be very distressing. In your professional life, you advance projects and tick tasks off an interminable to-do list. You feel successful, get credit and acknowledgment, and get paid. You could be unprepared for the significant and taxing shift that comes with switching to personal projects and a to-do list of things that only you will know about in retirement. When you aren't speaking to audiences about your job, closing that big deal, or earning the promotion you've been aiming for, you could feel less valuable and significant. When you eventually finish the home, family, and personal projects you didn't have time for while you were employed, you could feel satisfied. You probably won't understand what it's like to be retired until you do.

We do know that a record number of individuals are approaching retirement. The number of elderly people and their share of the population are rising in all countries, according to the World Health Organization (WHO). 1. According to WHO projections, one in six people worldwide will be over 60 by 2030, and by 2050, this number is predicted to have doubled.

Referred to as "population aging," this demographic trend entails a rise in the number of retirees and an increase in the average amount of time that individuals will be retired. Retirement is more than just not having a job; it may have a significant negative influence on your relationships, identity, and status. As a result, more people than ever are aging and living longer. It's not all gold, however. The data about the effect of stress on retirees' mental health is contradictory. A meta-analysis of 11 studies revealed that 28% of 6,111 retirees had depression. 2. According to one study, there is a 6% to 9% decline in mental health throughout an average six-year post-retirement period. There is also evidence that this impact may be greater for individuals who retire involuntarily, which makes sense given that controlling the terms of your retirement will likely be less stressful than feeling "forced out." 3. A different meta-analysis with 60 data sets and 557,111 participants showed that retirement lowered the incidence of depression by about 20%. 4 Lastly, a Harvard Medical School paper said that the symptoms of doing too little or too much in retirement might be the same: sleeplessness, sadness, anxiety, memory loss, and appetite loss. 5. High levels of ongoing stress are a risk factor and trigger for mental health illnesses, including anxiety and depression, even though these diseases are not usually the result of stress. Six Identifying your sources of stress can help you take proactive steps to prepare for this significant life transition from an emotional and psychological standpoint, helping you reduce and manage your stress and enjoy a more positive retirement—even though the research is contradictory and confusing and everyone has a different context.

Stress Factors

Naturally, how you handle the stress of this significant life event will depend on the specifics of your retirement. Your retirement-related stress may be caused by how you retire, how your daily routine changes, how it affects your relationships, how alone you feel, or financial worries.

How one retires

In a perfect world, we choose when and under what conditions to retire. You can experience more enthusiasm than worry or anxiety if you have made retirement plans and everything is going as planned. But not everyone can live up to that standard. You can go through a lot of stress since you were not prepared for having to retire earlier than you had hoped to due to sickness, having to care for family members, or being laid off.

Your daily schedule

The transition from a 40- to 60-hour workday to 40- to 60-hour free time may be difficult, particularly in the first few weeks or months after retirement, even if everything goes perfectly according to your plans or dreams. Even if you have planned your lessons, your vacations, and your hobbies, the difference in pace takes some getting used to.

Relationship modifications

Even if working from home became the norm for many due to the pandemic, you may feel alone and unconnected if you don't have a team to check in with and enjoy happy hours, watercooler talks about sports and the news, and business events with free drinks and snacks.

a sense of loneliness.

There's no denying that retirement may cause FOMO or the fear of missing out. You could question if you made the proper choice in retiring when you see your coworkers who are still employed traveling on business trips and receiving significant promotions. Additionally, if you live alone, as many seniors do, you can feel lonely now that you're not seeing people for work daily. In the United States, more seniors live alone than in any other country, according to Pew Research Center research. Of the 130 nations examined, 16% of people over 60 live alone, compared to 27% in the United States. 7. Due in part to women living longer and marrying older men, elderly women are almost twice as likely to live alone as their male counterparts. Furthermore, a large body of research demonstrates that social isolation has a detrimental effect on seniors' mental and physical health. 8

Money-related issues

Many individuals at various phases of life often experience stress related to money. When individuals retire and no longer have the opportunity to build their savings, their financial stress levels might rise. 37% of Americans feel unprepared or uncertain about whether they are on track for retirement, according to a CNBC report on the topic. 9. Having enough money to pay for health care expenses is a major problem, particularly for Americans, as our health inevitably deteriorates with age. According to a poll, over thirty percent of Americans worry that they won't have enough money for medical expenses in the next year. 10. You may be concerned about carrying debt into retirement if you still owe money on things like a mortgage or college loans (for you or your kids). Finally, a lot of individuals are concerned about whether their savings will last them the rest of their lives as life expectancy rises. And these anxieties are further made worse by the present economic downturn. It might also be upsetting to learn that, going forward, your expensive meals and travel would have to come from your fixed income if you were employed as an entertainer or traveler. Therefore, saving money for retirement is essential to maintaining your mental and emotional well-being.

Handling Stress Throughout Retirement's Phases

There are seven phases of retirement, according to Robert Atchley's seminal book The Sociology of Retirement, and the causes of stress might vary depending on where you are in the "retirement life cycle." 11 We'll go over the first six stages to assist you with retirement planning. Understanding the phases will enable you to recognize them and control your reaction during them. (We won't discuss the last phase, termination, which occurs when a person is nearing the end of their life.) Although each individual experiences these phases of retirement at their own rate and may skip some, such as the disillusionment and reorientation phases, depending on their outlook on life, most people go through them in the order that they are described. A shift in the environment may sometimes result in a leap forward or backward. For instance, receiving money later in life might push someone into the stability stage or back to their honeymoon phase. Alternatively, a more unfavorable event, such as receiving a chronic illness diagnosis, can trigger a transition to the disillusionment or reorientation stages.

Preretirement is the first phase. This often occurs five to ten years before your intended retirement date, since this is when most individuals begin to concentrate on their financial preparation. This might include moving into a smaller house after your kids have grown up. Others may need to make plans for relocating to a different area of the country. For instance, those who want to relocate permanently or temporarily (also known as snowbirds) to an area with a more temperate environment may do so if they reside somewhere with long, harsh winters. Stress related to this stage of your career might stem from generic worries about aging or becoming older, concerns about having enough money saved, and a lack of a clear retirement plan.

Cope: Put your attention on creating a precise and detailed strategy for the future to deal with this stressor. Put your retirement aspirations on paper, schedule a meeting with a financial planner to assess the viability of your plans, and start taking action to realize your ambitions. To prepare for a long and healthy retirement, it might also be beneficial to concentrate on eating and living a better lifestyle. To help you get ready for your new normal of retirement, Consuela Chapman, a certified therapist and wellness coach in North Carolina, suggests that you take advantage of any therapy provided via your company's employee assistance programs.

The retirement day stage is the second and shortest. This is the official day of your retirement, which your colleagues and company may be commemorating. It might indicate a present of some kind as well as an elegant dining experience or an office party. Since this day signifies the beginning and end of their professional careers, a lot of individuals look forward to it. Even though the actual day could be joyful, deciding on a date and alerting your family and employer might cause tension. And this day might not be as joyous for you if you feel like you're being pushed out.

Cope: The easiest approach to handling this day is to go back on your professional accomplishments. You might use this as the main topic of your retirement speech or the farewell email you write to coworkers. You may even achieve this solely for the satisfaction of knowing that you did it. As you bid farewell to work and begin a new chapter in your life, write a list of at least three things for which you are thankful as another method to make today as happy as possible.

The third stage is known as the honeymoon phase, during which you engage in many of the activities you have always wanted to but were unable to do due to time constraints or lack of freedom: spontaneous travel to visit family or discover new locations; complete indulgence in your hobbies, such as knitting, painting, or gardening; casual language learning; or volunteer work for a cause that is dear to your heart. During the honeymoon period, you could also like the feeling of losing things, like having an alarm clock to wake you up, a hard commute, or a schedule full of appointments that leaves you with little time for eating or coffee breaks. This phase has no set duration since it mostly depends on how you feel about retiring and how much you want to accomplish, both emotionally and psychologically.

Cope: Enjoy yourself; this is the least stressful time of retirement, which is why it's called the honeymoon phase. You may experience a sense of happiness, fulfillment, excitement, and accomplishment as you embrace retirement and the newfound life that you have worked so hard to attain. It could be beneficial to keep a record of your happy moments throughout this time, so you have something to fall back on when you need a pick-me-up as you transition into less happy times. Even when everything is going well, you may want to draft an advance directive in case anything goes wrong. "My number one piece of advice for retirees is to immediately identify who will be both your financial and your medical power of attorney, should you need someone to make decisions on your behalf, and who is going to help you get what you need if you are physically or cognitively unable to do it yourself," says Vanessa Souza, a social worker with more than 15 years of experience working with the elderly in the San Francisco Bay Area. An advance directive is simply one more option to have peace of mind in the future, but she discovers that most people don't want to worry about this while things are going well.

The disillusionment stage follows, during which you begin to question whether "this is it" for the rest of your life. As you have too much freedom and not enough structure, the emotional high of being able to do as you want begins to wear off. If you're not making money, you could start to worry about merely spending it. You can be met with fear rather than excitement on yet another unforeseen day. A goal or a sensation of achievement might be all you can think about. Additionally, as Chapman states, "Those who have recently retired and are finding it difficult to adjust to the new lifestyle may start to experience anxiety and/or depression." Retirees often experience the grieving cycle as well. It is a loss to give up a profession and the connections that were built.

Cope: Concentrating on the aspects of retirement that you love while attempting to address the aspects that you don't is one strategy to manage the stress of this stage. To help you get back into a more optimistic frame of mind, review your gratitude list, your list of professional accomplishments, and some of your honeymoon period diary entries. Engage in activities you both like doing as a family and take the initiative to connect with them. And if you miss collaborating with a fantastic group of people on a common objective, consider volunteering in a K–12 classroom, serving meals on wheels, or joining a charity board. These are just a few examples of volunteer opportunities where you can engage with others to improve someone's life. Retirees' physical and mental health has been shown to improve with hobbies and volunteer work. Twelve If you want to get out of your retirement rut, think about volunteering overseas or joining the Peace Corps. Additionally, seek out the assistance of a mental health expert to assist you in overcoming the chronic emotions of sadness and loss.

Reorientation is the sixth step. As you begin to adjust to your new identity and way of life, this phase can be the most difficult for some people. You want to feel purposeful in this new life you have made for yourself and be able to respond to the age-old question of what you do without experiencing any worry.

Cope: Establish a schedule that suits you to get through this phase. Maintain a regular sleep schedule, exercise to keep your bones and muscles strong, maintain a healthy weight, and lower your risk of chronic diseases. These practices may help you manage your circadian rhythms. To strengthen your emotional resilience and maintain social connections, you should also schedule frequent get-togethers with friends and family. Seek opportunities for meaningful community engagement to give your life meaning and purpose.

The stability stage, often referred to as the reconciliation stage, is the penultimate and last step that we will discuss here. You seem to have found a life that fulfills you and has meaning at this time. You will have emotional and psychological ups and downs like everyone else, but you have coping mechanisms to handle these shifts with ease. Retirement is a time of change in life, and like any other, there will be ups and downs in your psychological and emotional state. You could have to cope with a spouse or child's sickness, the loss of friends and relatives, or financial setbacks.

Cope: Rely on the coping mechanisms you established earlier in life that are effective for you. Alternate these tactics as necessary. At this point, you may want to think about writing down your life's narrative as a historical record or as a legacy for your kids or grandkids. You will feel more like you have left a legacy if you write or record your life's narrative. Furthermore, telling these tales to your loved ones and the community regularly helps strengthen your bonds. You may even consider writing and releasing a memoir.

No matter what stage of retirement you are in, you should seek the assistance of a mental health provider, or a leader in your faith community if you are involved in one, to help you through this important life transition if you are feeling overwhelmed or if you find that you are experiencing prolonged periods of anxiety, depression, or other mental health challenges. It will undoubtedly be difficult for you to get used to a whole different way of life after spending decades of your life working. No matter how your retirement turns out in the end, mentally and emotionally preparing for it can help lessen the stress it may cause and allow you to concentrate on living the life you've always wanted with a lasting feeling of purpose, fulfillment, and connection.

CHAPTER 6.

Set yourself up for success

How Are You Going to Assess Your Life?

There are seven phases of retirement, according to Robert Atchley's seminal book The Sociology of Retirement, and the causes of stress might vary depending on where you are in the "retirement life cycle." 11 We'll go over the first six stages to assist you with retirement planning. Understanding the phases will enable you to recognize them and control your reaction during them. (We won't discuss the last phase, termination, which occurs when a person is nearing the end of their life.) Although each individual experiences these phases of retirement at their own rate and may skip some, such as the disillusionment and reorientation phases, depending on their outlook on life, most people go through them in the order that they are described. A shift in the environment may sometimes result in a leap forward or backward. For instance, receiving money later in life might push someone into the stability stage or back to their honeymoon phase. Alternatively, a more unfavorable event, such as receiving a chronic illness diagnosis, can trigger a transition to the disillusionment or reorientation stages.

Preretirement is the first phase. This often occurs five to ten years before your intended retirement date, since this is when most individuals begin to concentrate on their financial preparation. This might include moving into a smaller house after your kids have grown up. Others may need to make plans for relocating to a different area of the country. For instance, those who want to relocate permanently or temporarily (also known as snowbirds) to an area with a more temperate environment may do so if they reside somewhere with long, harsh winters. Stress related to this stage of your career might stem from generic worries about aging or becoming older, concerns about having enough money saved, and a lack of a clear retirement plan.

Cope: Put your attention on creating a precise and detailed strategy for the future to deal with this stressor. Put your retirement aspirations on paper, schedule a meeting with a financial planner to assess the viability of your plans, and start taking action to realize your ambitions. To prepare for a long and healthy retirement, it might also be beneficial to concentrate on eating and living a better lifestyle. To help you get ready for your new normal of retirement, Consuela Chapman, a certified therapist and wellness coach in North Carolina, suggests that you take advantage of any therapy provided via your company's employee assistance programs.

The retirement day stage is the second and shortest. This is the official day of your retirement, which your colleagues and company may be commemorating. It might indicate a present of some kind as well as an elegant dining experience or an office party. Since this day signifies the beginning and end of their professional careers, a lot of individuals look forward to it. Even though the actual day could be joyful, deciding on a date and alerting your family and employer might cause tension. And this day may not be as joyous for you if you feel like you're being pushed out.

Cope: The easiest approach to handling this day is to go back on your professional accomplishments. You might use this as the main topic of your retirement speech or the farewell email you write to coworkers. You may even achieve this solely for the satisfaction of knowing that you did it. As you bid farewell to work and begin a new chapter in your life, write a list of at least three things for which you are thankful as another method to make today as happy as possible.

The third stage is known as the honeymoon phase, during which you engage in many of the activities you have always wanted to but were unable to do due to time constraints or lack of freedom: spontaneous travel to visit family or discover new locations; complete indulgence in your hobbies, such as knitting, painting, or gardening; casual language learning; or volunteer work for a cause that is dear to your heart. During the honeymoon period, you could also like the feeling of losing things, like having an alarm clock to wake you up, a hard commute, or a schedule full of appointments that leaves you with little time for eating or coffee breaks. This phase has no set duration since it mostly depends on how you feel about retiring and how much you want to accomplish, both emotionally and psychologically.

Cope: Enjoy yourself; this is the least stressful time of retirement, which is why it's called the honeymoon phase. You may experience a sense of happiness, fulfillment, excitement, and accomplishment as you embrace retirement and the newfound life that you have worked so hard to attain. It could be beneficial to keep a record of your happy moments throughout this time, so you have something to fall back on when you need a pick-me-up as you transition into less happy times. Even when everything is going well, you may want to draft an advance directive in case anything goes wrong. "My number one piece of advice for retirees is to immediately identify who will be both your financial and your medical power of attorney, should you need someone to make decisions on your behalf, and who is going to help you get what you need if you are physically or cognitively unable to do it yourself," says Vanessa Souza, a social worker with more than 15 years of experience working with the elderly in the San Francisco Bay Area. An advance directive is simply one more option to have peace of mind in the future, but she discovers that most people don't want to worry about this while things are going well.

The disillusionment stage follows, during which you begin to question whether "this is it" for the rest of your life. As you have too much freedom and not enough structure, the emotional high of being able to do as you want begins to wear off. If you're not making money, you could start to worry about merely spending it. You can be met with fear rather than excitement on yet another unforeseen day. A goal or a sensation of achievement might be all you can think about. Additionally, as Chapman states, "Those who have recently retired and are finding it difficult to adjust to the new lifestyle may start to experience anxiety and/or depression." Retirees often experience the grieving cycle as well. It is a loss to give up a profession and the connections that were built.

Cope: Concentrating on the aspects of retirement that you love while attempting to address the aspects that you don't is one strategy to manage the stress of this stage. To help you get back into a more optimistic frame of mind, review your gratitude list, your list of professional accomplishments, and some of your honeymoon period diary entries. Engage in activities you both like doing as a family and take the initiative to connect with them. And if you miss collaborating with a fantastic group of people on a common objective, consider volunteering in a K–12 classroom, serving meals on wheels, or joining a charity board. These are just a few examples of volunteer opportunities where you can engage with others to improve someone's life. Retirees' physical and mental health has been shown to improve with hobbies and volunteer work. Twelve If you want to get out of your retirement rut, think about volunteering overseas or joining the Peace Corps. Additionally, seek out the assistance of a mental health expert to assist you in overcoming the chronic emotions of sadness and loss.

Reorientation is the sixth step. As you begin to adjust to your new identity and way of life, this phase might be the most difficult for some individuals. You want to feel purposeful in this new life you have made for yourself and be able to respond to the age-old question of what you do without experiencing any worry.

Cope: Establish a schedule that suits you to get through this phase. Maintain a regular sleep schedule, exercise to keep your bones and muscles strong, maintain a healthy weight, and lower your risk of chronic diseases. These practices may help you manage your circadian rhythms. To strengthen your emotional resilience and maintain social connections, you should also schedule frequent get-togethers with friends and family. Seek opportunities for meaningful community engagement to give your life meaning and purpose.

The stability stage, often referred to as the reconciliation stage, is the penultimate and last step that we will discuss here. You seem to have found a life that fulfills you and has meaning at this time. You will have emotional and psychological ups and downs like everyone else, but you have coping mechanisms to handle these shifts with ease. Retirement is a time of change in life, and like any other, there will be ups and downs in your psychological and emotional state. You could have to cope with a spouse or child's sickness, the loss of friends and relatives, or financial setbacks.

Cope: Rely on the coping mechanisms you established earlier in life that are effective for you. Alternate these tactics as necessary. At this point, you may want to think about writing down your life's narrative as a historical record or as a legacy for your kids or grandkids. You will feel more like you have left a legacy if you write or record your life's narrative. Furthermore, telling these tales to your loved ones and the community regularly helps strengthen your bonds. You may even consider writing and releasing a memoir.

No matter what stage of retirement you are in, you should seek the assistance of a mental health provider, or a leader in your faith community if you are involved in one, to help you through this important life transition if you are feeling overwhelmed or if you find that you are experiencing prolonged periods of anxiety, depression, or other mental health challenges. It will undoubtedly be difficult for you to get used to a whole different way of life after spending decades of your life working. No matter how your retirement turns out in the end, mentally and emotionally preparing for it can help lessen the stress it may cause and allow you to concentrate on living the life you've always wanted with a lasting feeling of purpose, fulfillment, and connection.

Make your life a strategy

The idea of strategy definition and application is useful in addressing the second question: How can I make sure that my connection with my family proves to be a lasting source of happiness? Its main takeaway is that the kinds of projects that management funds define an organization's strategy. What comes out of a company's resource allocation process that is not skillfully handled may vary greatly from what management had in mind. Companies underinvest in projects that are essential to their long-term plans because their decision-making processes are set up to direct resources toward those that give the most observable and instantaneous rewards.

I've been following the lives of my 1979 HBS classmates over the years, and I've seen that an increasing number of them have been miserable, divorcing, and estranged from their kid's reunions. I promise you that not one of them graduated intending to intentionally get divorced and have children who would grow apart from them. And yet, a startlingly high percentage of them did just that. The cause? When deciding how to use their time, abilities, and energy, they failed to maintain their life's purpose at the forefront of their decisions.

The shocking thing is that a sizable portion of the 900 students that HBS selects from the finest in the world each year have never really considered what their life's purpose is. I informed the students that this may be their final opportunity to consider that subject in depth at HBS. They are insane if they believe that they will have more time and energy to contemplate later since life will only get more demanding: you take on a mortgage, put in 70 hours a week at work, and have kids and a spouse.

Having a distinct life purpose has been crucial for me. But I had to give it a lot of thought before I realized what it meant. I was in a very rigorous academic program as a Rhodes scholar, aiming to fit in an additional year of coursework during my time at Oxford. I decided to read, reflect, and pray for an hour each night about my purpose for being here on Earth. Maintaining that dedication was quite difficult for me since I wasn't learning applied econometrics for every hour I spent on it. Despite my doubts about my ability to pay for taking so much time off from school, I persisted and eventually discovered what my life's mission was.

I would have made a grave mistake in life if I had wasted that hour a day studying the newest methods for solving autocorrelation issues in regression analysis. I use econometrics tools sometimes, but I use my understanding of my life's mission daily. It's the most valuable lesson I've ever encountered. I assure my students that if they take the time to determine what their life's mission is, it will rank among the most significant discoveries they made while attending HBS. If they can't figure it out, they'll simply go out into the harsh waves of life without a rudder and be beaten up. The ability to clearly articulate their goal will take precedence over understanding the four Ps, the five forces, disruptive innovation, activity-based costing, balanced scorecards, and core competencies.

My religious convictions served as the foundation for my mission, but other things may guide someone. One of my former students, for instance, decided that his mission was to raise children who were as capable of being devoted to this cause and each other as he was and to bring honesty and economic success to his nation. Like me, he has family and people as his primary concerns.

Selecting and effectively pursuing a career is only one instrument in reaching your goals. But life might lose its meaning if it has no purpose.

Distribute your resources.

Your life's plan is ultimately shaped by the choices you make about how to spend your own time, effort, and skills.

I'm attempting to run several "businesses" that compete for these resources: I want to have wonderful children, have a fulfilling relationship with my wife, prosper professionally, give back to my church, and so on. And I have precisely the same issue that a business has. My time, energy, and ability are all restricted. How much time do I spend on each of these endeavors?

The decisions you make about allocation might cause your life to diverge significantly from your original plan. Opportunities that you never anticipated arise, and sometimes that's a wonderful thing. However, negative results may occur if your resources are misallocated. I can't help but feel that the problems of my former classmates, who unintentionally engaged in lives of empty sadness, are directly related to a short-term viewpoint.

Individuals with a strong drive for success, which encompasses all Harvard Business School alums, will instinctively devote any spare 30 minutes or additional energy to tasks that result in the greatest observable progress. The most tangible proof that we are progressing comes from our careers. You deliver a product, complete a design, wrap up a presentation, seal a deal, give a lecture, publish a paper, get paid, and advance in your career. Putting time and effort into your marriage and your kids, on the other hand, usually doesn't provide the same instant feeling of success. Children misbehave daily. You won't be able to put your hands on your hips and declare, "I raised a good son or a good daughter," until twenty years from now. You may put your spouse's relationship at risk, and things don't appear to be getting worse daily. Even though close, loving ties with family members are the most potent and long-lasting source of pleasure, people who are determined to succeed have an unconscious tendency to overinvest in their jobs and underinvest in their families.

Studying the underlying reasons for company failures again reveals this tendency toward projects that provide instant satisfaction. Applying that perspective to individual lives reveals the same startling and depressing trend: individuals are giving less and less money to the things they used to believe were most important.

Establish a Culture

Our lesson uses a key paradigm called the Tools of Cooperation, which essentially asserts that managing with vision isn't as easy as it seems. It is one thing to accurately predict the hazy future and map out the necessary course adjustments for the firm. However, it's a different story to convince staff members who may not be aware of the upcoming changes to align and collaborate to steer the business down that new path. Being able to use the right instruments to get the required collaboration is an essential management ability.

The theory arranges these instruments along two axes: the degree to which organization members concur on what they want to gain from their involvement in the venture and the degree to which they agree on the course of action that will lead to the intended outcomes. Use "power tools" (coercion, threats, punishment, and so on) to get cooperation when there is minimal agreement on both sides. This quadrant is where a lot of businesses begin, which is why the founding management team has to be so forceful in outlining the necessary steps and methods. When staff members consistently achieve success in collaborating to tackle certain duties, a consensus starts to emerge. Edgar Schein of MIT has referred to this procedure as how a culture is established. In the end, many don't even consider if the methods they use lead to success. They have established a culture because they adopt priorities and adhere to protocols more out of habit and assumption than out of conscious choice. Culture shapes the tried-and-true, socially acceptable ways in which group members deal with persistent issues in persuasive but unsaid ways. Furthermore, culture establishes the relative importance of various issue categories. It is a potentially effective managerial technique.

This model may be used to answer the following query: How can I make sure my family becomes a lasting source of happiness? My pupils rapidly discovered that power tools are the most basic instruments parents may use to coax cooperation from their kids. However, power tools stop working at some point throughout adolescence. At that moment, parents begin to wish that they had started working with their kids at a very early age to create a home culture where kids automatically follow their parents, treat others with respect, and make the correct decisions. Just as organizations have cultures, so do families. These cultures may develop unintentionally or deliberately.

Your children won't suddenly develop great self-esteem and the confidence to address challenging challenges in high school, even if you want them to have such traits. You must include them in your family's culture from the beginning. Children develop their self-esteem by taking on challenging tasks and discovering what works, just as workers do.

Steer clear of the "Marginal Costs" error.

In finance and economics, we are taught that while assessing different investments, we should not consider sunk or fixed costs but rather the marginal costs and revenues associated with each option. Our study teaches us that this concept encourages businesses to rely more on the systems they have already put in place to succeed than on helping them develop the skills they will need down the road. That strategy would work well if we were certain that the future would look precisely like the past. On the other hand, it is incorrect to act in this manner if the future differs, as it almost always does.

The final issue I pose to my students is how to live an honorable life (i.e., avoid going to prison). This theory answers that question. When we have to make moral decisions in our own lives, we often use the marginal cost theory without realizing it. A voice in our minds says, "Look, I know that most people shouldn't do something as a general rule. But this one time, in this specific extenuating scenario, it's OK. Whenever anything goes wrong "just this once," the marginal cost of it always seems enticingly cheap. It draws you in, and you never consider the full price of the decision or where that route would eventually go. The economics of "just this once" marginal cost justifies adultery and dishonesty in all of their forms.

I want to tell you a tale about how I realized in my own life the possible harm that may result from "just this once." I was a member of the varsity basketball team at Oxford University. We put in a ton of effort and were unbeaten at the end of the season. I've never had better buddies than the men on the team. We reached the last four in the British version of the NCAA tournament. It transpired that a Sunday was chosen to host the final game. At sixteen, I had personally promised God that I would never play ball on Sundays. I went to the coach and told him what was wrong. He couldn't believe it. As the starting center, my teammates were as well. Every player on the squad approached me and told me, "You have to play." Can't you disobey the rule just once, please?

Since I'm a devout guy, I went to pray and considered my options. I felt strongly that I should honor my pledge; therefore, I opted not to participate in the final game.

That was a minor choice, in many respects, involving one of my many thousands of Sundays. Theoretically, I could have stepped over the boundary once and refrained from doing so in the future. When I think back on it, however, one of the best choices I've ever made was to fight the urge to give in to the idea that, "In this exceptional situation, just this once, it's OK." Why? My life has been a never-ending series of fortunate events. If I hadn't stepped over the line that one time, I definitely would have in the years that followed.

This taught me that sticking to your values 98% of the time is far harder than sticking to them 100% of the time. You will be sorry for your decision if, like some of my previous students, you give in "just this once" after doing a marginal cost analysis. You must decide for yourself what your values are and draw the boundaries in a secure area.

Recall the Significance of Humility

This realization came to me when I was invited to Harvard College to give a course on humility. I asked each student to provide an example of the most modest person they had ever met. These modest individuals stood out for having a high degree of self-esteem. They were confident in who they were and knew who they were. We also concluded that humility is best described by how highly you value other people rather than by engaging in self-deprecating actions or attitudes. That type of humility naturally leads to good conduct. For instance, you would never steal from someone because you have an excessive amount of respect for them. You also wouldn't tell someone a falsehood.

Bringing humility into the world is essential. By the time you enroll in a prestigious graduate program, almost all of the knowledge you have acquired comes from superiors in your field—parents, instructors, and employers, for example. However, most of the individuals you'll see daily after graduating from Harvard Business School or any other prestigious university may not be wiser than you. And you'll have very few chances to learn if you think that only more intelligent individuals can teach you anything. Nonetheless, there are many possibilities for learning, provided you possess a little desire to pick up knowledge from everyone. Generally speaking, being modest requires feeling incredibly good about yourself and wanting to make those around you feel the same way. People who behave abusively, haughtily, or demeaningly toward others nearly always exhibit low self-esteem as a result of their conduct. To feel good about themselves, they must denigrate others.

Select the appropriate yardstick.

I received a cancer diagnosis this past year, and I had to consider the idea that I may not have long to live. Thankfully, it seems that I will escape unscathed. However, the event has given me a valuable perspective on my life.

I know I've had a significant influence because I can see how my ideas have helped the businesses that have utilized my research make large sums of money. But it's surprising to see how little that influence matters to me now that I've faced this illness. I've concluded that God will evaluate my life based on the unique lives I've touched rather than on financial gains.

That seems like the best course of action for all of us. Worry about the people you have assisted in becoming better people, not about the degree of personal notoriety you have attained. This is what I would advise you to do in the end: consider the yardstick by which your life will be measured and resolve to live each day in a way that will ultimately lead to a successful conclusion.

www.ingramcontent.com/pod-product-compliance
Lightning Source LLC
Chambersburg PA
CBHW072144290526
45794CB00004B/1411